This Study Belongs To:

_____

_____

_____

"Listen to the words of the wise; apply your heart to my instruction. For it is good to keep these sayings in your heart and always ready on your lips. I am teaching you today—yes, you—so you will trust in the LORD."

Proverbs 22:17-19.

Dear Sisters in Christ,

"Listen to the words of the wise; apply your heart to my instruction. For it is good to keep these sayings in your heart and always ready on your lips. I am teaching you today—yes, you—so you will trust in the LORD."
Proverbs 22:17-19 (NLT).

God is faithful to give us all we need for life and godliness (2 Peter 1:3). Its beginning is found in the fear of the Lord and seeking His ways above our own as we have seen in part 1 of this study.

The book of Proverbs is one of poetry and practical insight using a collection of contrasting and repetitive thoughts to point us to living the abundant life Jesus came to give. Not one of earthly and monetary riches, but the richness of a sound mind that brings glory to his name and peace to our soul.

If you studied Proverbs 1-17 with us, you began to see that walking in the wisdom of the world is trusting ourselves over Christ and can have devasting effects. Life experiences, positive or negative, often affect our ability to live with hearts and eyes of faith and the way to overcome the negative is to continually love the Lord with all our will.

Proverbs 18-31 will provide additional opportunities to surrender to the wisdom and Lordship of Jesus the Christ. He is wisdom personified in becoming the wisdom of God on our behalf (1 Corinthians 1:18-25). May we be strengthened and comforted in knowing that the fullness of the Godhead dwells in Christ.

Paul said it well:

"For in Him dwells all the fullness of the Godhead bodily; and you are complete in Him, who is the head of all principality and power."
Colossians 2:9-10.

The last half of this study will offer opportunities to search out your own hidden treasures of wisdom in the chapter being studied, and challenge you to go beyond the cross-references and questions posed by as you are led by the Holy Spirit and all you have learned in Part 1.

My hope and prayer is that each of us will continue to grow in understanding as we walk in the grace and knowledge of our Lord Jesus Christ so our lives will reflect the goodness of God to everyone we encounter along life's road.

In Christ,

Teresa

She
RAISES
Her
VOICE

PART TWO

Trusting God with All Your Will

"Listen to the words of the wise; apply your heart to my instruction. For it is good to keep these sayings in your heart and always ready on your lips. I am teaching you today—yes, you—so you will trust in the LORD."
Proverbs 22:17-19 (NLT).

Dedicated to all the women who have spoken into my life over the years and to those who desire wholeness and healing for their mind, body and soul. God's Word and wisdom is the foundation for understanding the truth about our value and purpose and living in his freedom to be the woman he created us to be.

May we trust God with our will.

"You shall know the truth and the truth shall make you free."
John 8:32.

Table of Contents

Introduction

This study is designed for individuals and groups. In each week there are 6 days of homework that will take approximately 15– 45 minutes a day to complete (depending on the level of study*). The 7th day is a day of reflection of the week's assignments, or for group study, the space can be used for discussion notes and to record praises and prayer requests that act as a journal.

The hope is that all students of the Bible will be encouraged—new or seasoned. We will study each proverb for two days. The first day will have: 1) **A Big Picture** view, with questions that promote overall instruction and application, and 2) **A Deeper Reflection** section that will include cross references designed to challenge our thinking and gain additional insights. The second day we will look at the chapter from **Another View** drawing on other passages for further discernment in walking in the Spirit (Galatians 5:16). Do what is comfortable and what time allows, though it is good to push our comfort levels as we move through each week.

The goal is to become well acquainted with each chapter and its wisdom for daily living. Therefore, there will be multiple occasions when the instructions direct a 2nd and sometimes 3rd reading of the same passages of Scripture along with the cross-references throughout. Most of the proverbs discuss the same topics, however, they tend to speak directly to the heart, mind or soul. It's fitting considering the Lord created us a triune being in his image. This will be the primary focus as we learn to love and trust God with all our will in greater ways.

I encourage you to resist the temptation to use a commentary and rely on the text and noted cross-references instead. It can be helpful to use a dictionary or a thesaurus to look up key words to gain better understanding. Let the Holy Spirit reveal the message to your spirit. We grow best by allowing Scripture to interpret Scripture and leaning into continual prayer.

Included in each *Day* will be a **Something to Consider** and **Something to Pray** section at the beginning of each proverb, and a **Closing Thought** at the end of the **Another View** section.

A message to group facilitators:

May the Lord lead you as you seek him for personal insight and in supporting the women in the group.

If you are stepping out in faith and leading a group for the first time, I applaud your courage and obedience to follow what God has placed in your heart.

When he calls, he directs. I encourage you to prepare a minimum of two weeks in advance. The first week for personal prayer, study and understanding; ask the Lord: What do you want to teach me for my relationship with you? The second week is to reflect on your answers, get better acquainted with all the passages and questions, and incorporate prayer for the women in your group—even if you are not quite sure who they are at this point. Ask the Lord to speak through you as you guide the conversation and gently lead the conversation back to the subject if it strays.

A message to participants:

Whatever your level of comfort, do not be discouraged. Complete what you are able, and the Lord will meet you right where you are and grow your understanding as you continue to seek him. Always begin the study with prayer asking the Holy Spirit to teach you what He has for you in this season of life. If you are participating in a group, you will have an opportunity to learn from others. Keep the faith!

May the Lord bless your faithfulness as you fellowship and grow into a woman of great wisdom through the power of the Holy Spirit and choose to trust God with all your will. Amen.

- **LEVEL 1:** 15-25 minutes – *The Big Picture* section of the first day of the proverb being studied.
- **LEVEL 2:** Roughly 45 minutes – *The Big Picture* and *Deeper Reflection* section of the first day.
- **SECOND DAY:** Roughly 30 minutes to complete the *Another View* section.

Group facilitators should be prepared to lead through all the assignments.

If you would like additional support or have any questions, write to me at Teresa @ riseupcfw.com. You are invited to join our on-line private Facebook group for women, Rise Up – CFW, Inc. – Interactive, at the following link: https://www.facebook.com/share/g/19xJMjN1Gm

Preparation

Before you begin, it is important to prepare your heart to receive all the Lord has for you. We are called to be transformed into the image of Christ by the renewing of our mind (Romans 12:2). One of the ways we can do this is by asking God to challenge our current understanding and give us new insights to his living word, then respond with a commitment to act upon what he reveals to us (See Psalm 119:33-40).

List at least two commitments you will make to the Lord as he faithfully answers your prayer to grow in the grace and knowledge of the Lord Jesus Christ.

1)

2)

I encourage writing a letter to the Lord. Seal it and tuck it away somewhere safe. After completing this study, open it and read it. You will be blessed by the ways God brought you closer to him in trust, peace and greater knowledge of his character.

Week One

She LEADS To JUSTICE

Proverbs 18-20

Day 1 - Proverbs 18

Something to Consider

Proverbs 18 can be called the Proverb of Fools in my opinion. Most of the verses build a case and recipe for an arrogant lack of insight, but others, how to find protection under the shelter of God's wings (Psalm 91:4).

Arrogance begins with isolation from the ways of God and his people:

"Whoever isolates himself seeks his own desire; he breaks out against all sound judgment."

Proverbs 18:1 (ESV).

For the non-believer, this pattern grows into wickedness and contempt for wisdom and for the God of all creation. Without repentance, it leads to a fruitless life on earth and ultimately, eternal separation from God in the lake of fire.

When we, as believers, pull away, we fall into the trap of the enemy and become fools though we are children of God. Because of his mercy and grace, however, he pulls us out of the pit and sets us back on the path that leads to safety.

"The name of the LORD is a strong tower; the righteous run into it and they are safe."

Proverbs 18:10.

Our big picture focus will be on the consequences of "freedom" and "independence" disguised as rewards for the foolish.

Something to Pray

Father, thank you for keeping me in your care and leading me back to yourself when I go astray. Help me to be a source of encouragement to others when they are going through a tough season. In the name of Jesus, amen.

Proverbs 18
The Big Picture

Read Proverbs chapter 18, then answer the following questions.

1) List 3 statements about fools as described by character and behavior. Consider all the synonyms for a foolish/wicked person.

Example: Isolator = feeds selfishness and rejects sound judgment

a.

b.

c.

2) List 2 examples of verse 3 in action.

a.

b.

3) Give an example of verse 17 in action.

4) List 3 positive statements you see, and how they encourage you.

a.

b.

c.

Deeper Reflection

"It is not good to be partial to the wicked or to deprive the righteous of justice."

Proverbs 18:5.

Proverbs 18:5 is an echo of the teaching throughout the Bible on partiality, favoritism, unjust weights, and calling good evil and evil, good.

This statement has a lot of practical lessons and applications from which to draw. Think about times in your life whether at home or in the workplace where favoritism has been in play...it doesn't feel good when on the receiving end, and yet there are times when we can be doing the same thing to others inadvertently, or blatantly. One of the first things that came to my mind is how I can have more grace for a non-believer than a believer, or a friend or stranger over my husband.

It's a natural part of our fallen nature, and is directly connected to our own fears, guilt or shame. We wound others out of our own woundedness. The reverse can also be true by being too hard on the wicked and not in right judgment toward the godly. As believers, however, this shouldn't be our practice and if we don't repent and turn from it, we will reap the consequences. The first being sinning against God, and the fallout from that can strain or cost us our relationships.

"A brother offended is harder to win than a strong city, and contentions are like the bars of a castle."

Proverbs 18:19.

Some of the best ways to avoid hurting others are to avoid favoritism, give credit where credit is due, and always stand in truth when it comes to evil and good.

Let's spend a little more time today focusing on passages that speak to these forms of evil behavior.

1) Read the following passages. Note how they add insight to Proverbs 18:5 and 18:19. Note the consequence of such behavior and from where it might stem.

a. Colossians 3:25:

b. 1 Timothy 5:21:

C. James 2:1-9:

2) Give 2 examples of partiality (grace and judgment) being shown to the wicked that we see in the world today.

3) How are you challenged by the above passages?

4) Is there an area of favoritism in your life that you need to move away from in repentance and behavior? What is it and what is your plan to be right with God?

Close out the day with prayer and reflection. Record additional insights you discovered that were not addressed in the assignment.

"You shall not show partiality in judgment; you shall hear the small as well as the great; you shall not be afraid in any man's presence, for the judgment is God's..."

Deuteronomy 1:17a-b.

Day 2 – Proverbs 18 – Another View

Something to Consider

"The name of the LORD is a strong tower; the righteous run into it and are safe."

Proverbs 18:10.

When I was a kid, we used to play a game called slaughterhouse. This game was played on a handball court. The object was to take out as many people as possible while all players ran for the safety of the wall. The goal was to be faster than everyone else so that you continued to be the one throwing the ball instead of being hit by it. It is like dodge ball, but one-sided. The runners could not throw the ball back, their only saving grace was to make it to the wall.

Looking back at this game as an adult, I see how unfair it was—not to mention mean-spirited. The ball wasn't thrown lightly. We all walked away with red marks, but we had fun, nonetheless. There was a sense of pride in knowing you could take the most hits and stay standing...

Which leads me to why this game came to mind as I think about Proverbs 18:10.

We have an enemy whose sole aim is to destroy those God created in his own image. The unsaved for eternity, the saved, this side of heaven. He relishes the ability to render God's children defeated and useless. Satan throws his fiery darts as fast and hard as he is able and he uses others to do it. He is relentless and when we try to fight him on our own and in our pride, we will walk around with bruises all over our hearts, minds and souls.

We have an incredible offering set before us and that is to run into the strong tower of the Lord so that we will be safe. The fiery darts won't stop coming, the difference is that in the LORD, the enemy's tactics will not penetrate to a crippling degree. We will be able to stand in the truth and know that we are secure in what God has done for us through Christ Jesus. In this, sorrow is turned to joy, and ashes are turned to beauty. The catch is, you and I need to be willing to run to his shelter instead of taking the blows as if we have no choice.

Today we will look at several promises of protection that come with walking in Christ.

Something to Pray

Father, give me the courage to run into your strong tower instead of standing frozen while the darts fly my way. Give me eyes to see others who need encouragement and use me to help them run to you. In the name of Jesus, amen.

Proverbs 18 – Another View

1) Read the following passages and note how they add insight to Proverbs 18:10.

a. 2 Samuel 22:31-33:

c. Psalm 59:16:

d. John 10:28-30:

2) Read Isaiah 2:22 and Jeremiah 17:5. What is the warning on trusting/ fearing people rather than the Lord?

3) Think of a time when you feared or were tempted to fear others instead of trusting God. What was the situation and the outcome of that choice and what would you do differently going forward?

4) Think about a time when you trusted God in a difficult situation. What was the outcome? How has that affected your walk with God?

Proverbs 18 – Closing Thoughts

"A man who has friends must himself be friendly, but there is a friend who sticks closer than a brother."

Proverbs 18:24.

    God is the only one just and merciful. He's the one that sticks closer than a brother in good times and when life hits hard.

    His justice through wisdom is seen throughout this chapter, providing earthly and heavenly examples for us.

    In our humanity, and especially as women, we are prone to live by our emotions and what makes us feel good. We eat "food" that tastes good and satisfies our temporary needs and we look to others to validate our life and feelings, but in the end, we are left empty and wanting more. Are we taking more than giving? Do we have unreasonable expectations of others, yet have little to offer in return?

    When we choose to run to the Lord, and stay with him, we will have peace and the ability to be the friend who sticks closer than a brother this side of heaven; for the married, the good gift to their husbands God says they can be.

    Let's choose to stick with our heavenly Father and Brother so we will be women who remember that there are always two sides to every story (Provers 18:13 & 17), and act justly in every situation.

"You will keep him in perfect peace, whose mind is stayed on You, because he trusts in You.

Isaiah 26:3.

    What other thoughts come to your mind? Write them down and share them with the group.

Related passages: Job 6:14; Ecclesiastes 4:9-12; Titus 3:1-2

Close out the day with prayer and reflection. Record additional insights you discovered that were not addressed in the assignment.

"The name of the LORD is a strong tower; the righteous run into it and are safe."

Proverbs 18:10.

What is the LORD's name? "Tell the people, I AM has sent you." Exodus 3:14.
• I AM merciful
• I AM Gracious
• I AM the way
• I AM truth
• I AM life
No wonder, he is our strong tower. We are safe in him. Thank you, Lord.

Day 3 — Proverbs 19

Something to Consider

INTEGRITY = Honesty, strong moral principles, moral uprightness, being whole and undivided

RESPONSIBILITY = Duty to deal with something or someone, being dependable, making good choices with what or who is entrusted to your care

ACCOUNTABILITY = being honest and dealing with bad choices/behavior and making amends or improvements, good communication

CONSEQUENCE = a negative result or effect on an action taken that is felt immediately or has lasting effects.

Proverbs 19 adds a layer to its contrasting statements related to the behavior of the wise and foolish, as well as real versus phony relationships by revealing another side of financial lack and gain, literal and spiritual. In previous chapters, being poor was connected to laziness and wealth to a hard and honest worker.
In this chapter, verse 1 sets the stage for all that follows:

"Better is the poor who walks in his integrity than one who is perverse in his lips and is a fool."

Proverbs 19:1.

The message here is that if having wealth costs us our integrity, then we are better off being poor. It doesn't imply settling for, or that poverty is a more noble route, it means that integrity must be elevated in status and understood as advantageous to our lives. Having integrity requires humility, which leads to peace with God. And in turn, it leads to rich and genuine relationships instead of shallow and phony interactions as we see throughout this chapter.

Something to Pray

Father, thank you for grace that measures my status by integrity and faithfulness to you, rather than the world's standard. Help me to see areas where I may be lacking in being genuine and the reasons why so that I can turn those areas over to you and live a life of integrity in greater ways in my thoughts and heart, not just in action. In the name of Jesus, amen.

Proverbs 19
The Big Picture

Read Proverbs chapter 19, then answer the following questions.

1) What do you learn about integrity and genuine relationships?

2) What do you learn about phony relationships?

3) What do you learn about false witnesses? What do you believe is the reason for the statement being made twice?

4) How do you see integrity and discretion working together in healthy relationships?

5) What do you learn about consequences and accountability?

6) How are you challenged by Proverbs 19?

Deeper Reflection

"Cease listening to instruction, my son, and you will stray from the words of knowledge."

Proverbs 19:27.

Distraction is one of the enemy's greatest tools and makes each of us susceptible to falling away from godly instruction. We can grow indifferent toward God's Word and find ourselves not praying or studying as we once did.

I am reminded of the many times I have left the dryer door open because I was distracted by another item on the list of chores only to have a house half cleaned, leaving me exhausted from running all over the place. Unfinished. Have you ever done something similar?

This reminder from Solomon is essential and has a layer of reprimand in it. To cease listening, we must be distracted by something that appears a higher priority, or perhaps it's a reflection of our hearts growing indifferent and prideful with a conscious or subconscious thought that we already know it and have heard it a thousand times. Take this study, for instance. It can be a good indicator of where we are given Proverbs is the most repetitive book in the entire Bible. What are your thoughts?

We have many examples in the Old Testament of this happening, and Jesus warned that the hearts of his followers would grow cold and cautioned us through Paul that we should not grow weary in well-doing.

Pride is at the root of all temptation to stop listening. In fact, we see it with Solomon. For all his warnings in 29 of the 31 chapters of Proverbs, he fell away from wisdom and went from being an example and encouragement to a rebellious cynic that we read about in Ecclesiastes.

"Whatever my eyes desired I did not keep from them. I did not withhold my heart from any pleasure, for my heart rejoiced in all my labor; and this was my reward from all my labor. Then I looked on all the works that my hands had done and on the labor in which I had toiled; and indeed all was vanity and grasping for the wind. There was no profit under the sun."

Ecclesiastes 2:10-11.

Let's spend a little more time looking at the dangers of pride and growing indifferent toward God.

1) Read the following passages and note how they add insight to Proverbs 19:27.

a. Jeremiah 9:23-24:

b. Matthew 24:12:

c. Revelation 3:14-21:

2) How are you challenged by the above references?

3) What is one thing you can do to look beyond what you already know?

Close out the day with prayer and reflection. Record additional insights you discovered that were not addressed in the assignment.

"And let us not grow weary while doing good, for in due season we shall reap if we do not lose heart."

Galatians 6:9.

Day 4 - Proverbs 19 - Another View

Something to Consider

"Hot-tempered people must pay the penalty. If you rescue them once, you will have to do it again."

Proverbs 19:19 (NLT).

I'll never forget my mom's words: "If you ever land yourself in jail, don't expect me to bail you out. If you get arrested, you probably deserve it."

The words seemed cold, but as I grew up and got into trouble (though never arrested), I realized she was right. "You can learn the easy way, or the hard way," she would say. And learn the hard way, I did. But the point is I learned. Several of my friends had parents cover for them time and again and they ended up worse off because there was no consequence.

We see this today across the board. Many do not accept responsibility for their actions and always blame others. Even the legal system, at times, sides with the offender over the officer or actual victim, treating them as if they are the victim.

God set a universal law in place that states there are consequences for sin. They are designed out of his love for his creation so that when they experience hardship, they will go to him in repentance for salvation and restoration.

Sometimes we get in God's way in our efforts to rescue. This is especially true with a loved one because we don't want to see them suffer. The truth is they will suffer far greater consequences if we don't love them enough to let them learn.

Today we will focus on God's law of sowing and reaping and the benefit of learning to stand on our own two feet.

Something to Pray

Heavenly Father, give me discernment from your Word and in any circumstances that will cause me to enable if I step in to help. Help me entrust my loved ones into your care so that they will see their need for you and cry out in repentance instead of relying on me to rescue or attempt to fix their situation. In the name of Jesus, amen.

Proverbs 19-Another View

1) Read the following passages and note how they add insight to Proverbs 19:19.

a. Job 4:7-8:

b. 1 Corinthians 5:1-8:

c. Galatians 6:5-8:

d. 1 John 5:16:

2) Read 2 Corinthians 7:1-11. Together with the above passages, what do you learn about the importance and power of personal responsibility and tough love?

3) How does this challenge any tendencies you have to rescue others? Could there be a deeper motive behind the rescue?

4) What new insights have you gained from Proverbs chapter 19, and what will you do to exercise additional wisdom going forward?

Proverbs 19 – Closing Thoughts

"People ruin their own lives by their own foolishness and then are angry with God."

Proverbs 19:3 (NLT).

"Let no one say when he is tempted, "I am tempted by God"; for God cannot be tempted by evil, nor does He Himself tempt anyone. But each one is tempted when he is drawn away by his own desires and enticed."

James 1:13-14.

As previously mentioned, this chapter is all about integrity and accountability. It's interesting how since sin entered in, the natural reaction is to blame God for our sinful choices. We blame him if we don't hear him, yet we don't read his Word. Or we ask why this or that happened and why he didn't intervene.

Perhaps the right question to ask ourselves is if our decision and choice was emotionally driven. We hear it all the time, and I've been guilty in years past of saying, "I feel in my heart that God is good with this. Or I have peace about this decision." But when compared to the Scriptures, I found my feelings and heart were not aligned at all.

Our heart is only trustworthy if we are walking in the Spirit, not led by feelings that contradict truth, but by the wisdom and knowledge of Christ. We must remember that Satan can and will give a false sense of peace by way of smooth and enticing lies as we learned in Proverbs chapter 8. Called son of the morning, he can disguise himself as an angel of light.

May we walk in integrity and strengthen our understanding of God's character and never tire of searching for wisdom as our prized possession because through her we find the grace, mercy, truth and justice of God.

When we do justly and love mercy, we will be women who give refreshing water to the soul of another. The alternative is to be an annoying and steady drip of criticism and judgment. Who needs that in their life? I don't want to be a continual dripping (Proverbs 19:13b). Do you?

Related passages: Psalm 106:3; Isaiah 30:18; Amos 5:24; Matthew 7:12

Close out the day with prayer and reflection. Record additional insights you discovered that were not addressed in the assignment.

"Now then, let the fear of the LORD be upon you. Be careful what you do, for there is no injustice with the LORD our God, or partiality or taking bribes."

2 Chronicles 19:7 (ESV).

Day 5 - Proverbs 20

Something to Consider

The overarching theme of this chapter is influence. We are all under the influence of something or someone—good or evil. Verse 1, cleverly and Holy Spirit placed, sets the stage for all that follows.

Alcohol is often referred to as spirits and has its origins in how alcohol is processed, below is a brief explanation as sited on Google:

> • The term "spirits" is used for distilled alcoholic beverages due to historical and alchemical connections to the concept of "spirit" as an essence or vital force. Early alchemists viewed distillation as a process of extracting the "spirit" or essence of a substance, particularly in the context of creating alcoholic beverages. The word "spirit" itself originates from the Latin "spiritus," meaning breath, breeze, or soul, and was used to describe the vapors produced during chemical processes like distillation.
> • Alchemical Origins: The term "spirit" in relation to alcohol stems from alchemy, where distillation was seen as a process of separating the "spirit" or volatile essence of a liquid. This process was believed to extract the most valuable and potent part of the substance.
> • Etymology: The word "spirit" comes from the Latin "spiritus," which encompasses breath, breeze, and soul. This connection to breath and the soul is significant because it links the concept of a vital force or essence to the distilled liquid.

"So be careful how you live. Don't live like fools, but like those who are wise. Make the most of every opportunity in these evil days. Don't act thoughtlessly, but understand what the Lord wants you to do. Don't be drunk with wine, because it will ruin your life. Instead be filled with the Spirit."

Ephesians 5:15-18 (NLT).

Notice the deceptive similarity to the truth of being led by the Spirit of God? May we stay away from harmful influence and ungodly behavior.

Something to Pray

Heavenly Father, be my only influence and draw me back with conviction when I am tempted to go my own way or let my emotions keep me from plowing the ground of my heart with your Word. In the name of Jesus, amen.

Proverbs 20
The Big Picture

Read Proverbs chapter 20, then answer the following questions.

1) List the influences you see, explicit or implied in this chapter.

2) List the verses that speak to justice.

3) What is your understanding of verse 20? What would this mean for those who had/have emotionally or physically abusive parents?

4) What attributes of God do you see throughout the chapter?

5) Which verse/s challenge you most and why?

6) Who or what has a greater influence on you in this season of life? Give an example.

Deeper Reflection

"The lazy man will not plow because of winter; He will beg during harvest and have nothing."

Proverbs 20:4.

LAZY = Idle. Unwilling to work or use energy. Lack motivation.
SYNONYMS = Sluggish. Listless. Dull. Neglect.

The practicality of this verse is clear, and farmers would understand what is being said. It shouldn't matter how we feel about something, what matters is that we remain diligent to do the work, or we will find ourselves lacking necessities.

It seems it wasn't much different back then, but the idea of being led by our feelings has increased at an alarming rate and has increased in the body of Christ even though feelings have never been factored into obedience and a diligent walk with God in the entire Bible.

Perpetual laziness can become a spiritual stronghold and leave us without strength and the necessary "food" needed to live a faithful life when we cave to its emotional pull. We are called to plow, and if necessary, do it with our feelings in tow. To do this, we must decide to surrender our will and emotions to God and trust that his grace will meet us right where we are.

Many times, laziness is a symptom of something deeper: hopelessness, or self-pity, which is also a symptom of a bruised ego for not getting our own way, or something more serious like unresolved wounds.

When we find ourselves too lazy or too tired to pray or eat of God's Word, let's remind ourselves that's when we need it most. We shouldn't let feelings lead us to believe we can't do something. In Christ, there is no such thing as "can't". It's a choice: I will or I won't. I want to, or I don't. Once we decide, we can seek support through godly counselors to work through the why's and wounds so that laziness loses its grip. May we be women of godly discipline and set an example to the hurting that Christ is bigger than our feelings.

"...But I discipline my body and bring it into subjection, lest, when I have preached to others, I myself should become disqualified."

1 Corinthians 9:27.

Let's spend a little more time looking into Scriptures that challenge us to be strengthened in the power of God's might, and the dangers of spiritual laziness.

1) Read the following passages and note how they add insight to Proverbs 20:4.

a. Matthew 26:40-43:

b. 2 Timothy 2:15:

c. Hebrews 12:12:

2) Is there anything hindering you from seeking the Lord in full measure in this season of your life? What is one step you can take to walk in the Spirit for growth?

3) How does a fresh understanding of some of the causes of spiritual laziness give you increased compassion and grace for others? What will you do differently when you encounter a sister who seems lazy or looks like they just don't care?

Close out the day with prayer and reflection. Record additional insights you discovered that were not addressed in the assignment.

"Do not be deceived: Evil company corrupts good habits. Awake to righteousness, and do not sin; for some do not have the knowledge of God. I speak this to your shame."

1 Corinthians 15:33.

Day 6 – Proverbs 3 – Another View

Something to Consider

As much as I try and pray to be pure in my decisions and judgments, I'm not capable of dividing truth from error 100% of the time for myself. Nor am I able to weigh the heart and thoughts of others, and yet I do this more than I care to admit. What about you?

We are to extend grace and provide godly encouragement to others, not judge their heart or question their salvation. That is between them and God. The only way we will be able to change this prideful behavior, is to fully believe and trust that God is God and we are not. Theoretically, we believe this, but in practice, it's a challenge. Thankfully, we have 6 reminders in Proverbs 20 regarding the role of kings and more importantly, the Lord.

"The hearing ear and the seeing eye, the LORD has made them both."
Proverbs 20:12.

Who better to know and judge than the Lord, our almighty maker? He judges righteously and graciously. His justice is pure and we can count on him to repay evil, restore hope and lead those who follow his ways. Hallelujah and amen to that!

Today we will focus on God as our merciful king who reigns and upholds his throne and what we can learn. As we do, may we continue to choose to love and trust the Lord our God with all our will.

"Mercy and truth preserve the king, and by lovingkindness he upholds his throne.
Proverbs 20:28.

Something to Pray

Father, free me from any tendencies to unjustly judge others. Keep me in step with your Holy Spirit that reminds me I don't have all the facts, and I too have areas of need and healing in my life. I commit to extending grace in greater ways as I learn more about your character. In the name of Jesus, amen.

Proverbs 20 – Another View

Read the following passages. Note how they add insight to God's character and his ways.

a. Proverbs 20:26-27:

b. Matthew 13:24-43:

g. 1 Corinthians 3:11-15:

2) What have you been reminded of, or learned about God's character in this section? List them.

3) What part of your will is challenged by these passages? Which stands out the most and why?

Proverbs 3 – Closing Thought

"Most men will proclaim each his own goodness, but who can find a faithful man?"

Proverbs 20:6.

When I think about where I was 40 years ago, it's easy for me to proclaim I am a pretty good person. From my youth to where I am now, the difference is night and day. When I consider the goodness of God and his faithfulness, however, I'm reminded that I still have a long road ahead in the transformation process.

I continue to learn that when I try in my own strength to be more like Christ, I not only fail, I also get easily frustrated. It doesn't take long to recognize it's because my focus shifted back to self and my own standards and away from being strong in the power of Christ, which causes me to cut off the flow of the Holy Spirit.

We are told not to quench the Spirit (1 Thessalonians 5:19) or grieve him (Ephesians 4:30).

Nancy Missler, one of the most influential women in my life, never failed to remind her readers that it's a moment-by-moment choice to surrender our thought life to Christ and allow him to live through us. I am challenged by this reminder after studying this chapter. How about you? God is justice and mercy, let's leave the judgment to him.

"You have a mighty arm; strong is Your hand, righteousness and justice are the foundation of our throne; mercy and truth go before Your face."

Psalm 89:13-14.

I pulled out a study I did in 1991 on the Book of Proverbs called, *"Woman of Wisdom"* by Myrna Alexander. In her lesson on Proverbs 20, she had this to say:

> The emphasis of Proverbs is to drive us to a continual decision. What will I do with this truth; how can this be applied to my life? We are not allowed to remain hearers only; a wise woman is driven to make a decision to be a doer of His Word if her path is to shine "ever brighter till the full light of day" (Provers 4:18).

Today, let's decide to let the Spirit lead and follow wisdom's way of justice. Let's decide to put on Christ daily by surrendering our will to the influence of the Holy Spirit every moment of every day. Amen? Amen.

Close out the day with prayer and reflection. Record additional insights you discovered that were not addressed in the assignment.

"Let love be without hypocrisy. Abhor what is evil. Cling to what is good. Be kindly affectionate to one another with brotherly love in honor giving preference to one another; not lagging in diligence, fervent in spirit, serving the Lord; rejoicing in hope, patient in tribulation, continuing steadfastly in prayer; distributing to the needs of the saints, given to hospitality."

Romans 12:9-13.

Day 7

Reflect on this week's assignments and note any additional thoughts below. For group studies, choose 1 or 2 questions from each day and discuss as a group and record your thoughts and/or prayer requests.

Week Two

She GIVES Clear VISION

Proverbs 21-23

Day 1 – Proverbs 21

Something to Consider

SOVEREIGNTY = Supreme power and/or authority. Rightful status. Independent
SYNONYMS = Dominion, predominance, jurisdiction.

Wisdom reveals the sovereignty of God in this chapter. Our spiritual eyes are given insight into behavior; our motives and those of others are made clear. This is not revealed so we can judge and criticize others but rather give us opportunity to repent and turn from our ways as God leads us in his. It's a call to remember that he is the one who sees the heart and is the only one who has the authority to judge.

The gift of freewill won't negate his sovereignty, nor does it mean he surrenders it to our will. This is one of the many reasons for the reminder throughout the Bible that we need to fear the Lord and not the enticement of sin (the immoral woman). He is our creator, our light and our salvation. Not only for our eternal destination, but for everyday living.

"People may be right in their own eyes, but the LORD examines the heart."
Proverbs 21:2.

"The LORD's light penetrates the human spirit, exposing every hidden motive."
Proverbs 20:27.

His light exposes all we cannot see so that we can be at peace with him as we live out our lives. That light is also the living water that fills and is intended to overflow and lead us in the way we should go.

As you read this chapter, consider God's perfect will, and his permissive will, which is simply granting us the freedom to make our own choices even when they don't align with his. Understanding this aspect of the Lord's character gives us insight into why people do what they do.

Something to Pray

Father, thank you for the gift of choice, please help me use it wisely so I follow your direction instead of my own. In the name of Jesus, amen.

Proverbs 21
The Big Picture

1) List every characteristic of God that you see in Proverbs 21.

2) What is most acceptable to the Lord, and what is the opposite of it?

3) List 3 acts of righteousness that are mentioned in this chapter, and the verse you found them in. NOTE: Some acts of righteousness and justice are found to be the opposite of what is said of the wicked. How do these encourage or challenge you?

a.

b.

c.

4) What is the desirable treasure referred to in Proverbs 21:20?

5) What principle listed in this chapter challenges you most and what will you do to walk in wisdom in greater ways?

Deeper Reflection

"Better to dwell in a corner of a housetop, than in a house shared with a contentious woman."

Proverbs 21:9.

"Better to dwell in the wilderness, than with a contentious and angry woman."

Proverbs 21:19.

Twice. Solomon says this twice so it's worth pondering.

I wonder how many wives he had at that time. Was it wife number 1, 15, or had he accumulated 1000 by this time? How many influential women did he have in his life? What was his mother like? Aunts, grandmothers, sisters? My guess is it probably doesn't matter because 1 contentious woman in his life would be enough. It certainly is for me. How about you?

In those days rooftops were flat with no place of refuge. Anyone on a rooftop would be fully exposed to the weather. The beating hot sun, or frigid air. It would be the same in the wilderness. Not the beautiful wilderness surrounded by streams and gorgeous trees like in the northwest, but the deserted wilderness where there is no escape from the weather and dust. Are you getting a vivid image in your mind? It's better. Far better than being anywhere near a woman who has a pattern of being contentious.

The upside to Solomon's statement is the testament to the power a woman has to affect her environment—home, work and community at large. God created women to be helpers. Not less than, but with a set of different skills to bring balance. A wise woman will know when it's time to be silent and time to speak up. A wise woman will know when it's time to follow and time to lead. All without lording, or complaining, and examining ourselves daily to make sure we are in the faith, operating in the power of the Holy Spirit.

"Examine yourselves as to whether you are in the faith. Test yourselves. Do you not know yourselves, that Jesus Christ is in you?—unless indeed you are disqualified."

2 Corinthians 13:5.

"Let your speech always be with grace, seasoned with salt, that you may know how you ought to answer each one."

Colossians 4:6.

Let's spend a little more time looking at a few examples of women in Scripture, the power they had and what difference they made—for better or for worse.

1) Read the following passages. Note all you see about the wisdom or wickedness used in the situation and the outcome.

Delilah
a. Judges 16:

Abigail
b. 1 Samuel chapter 25:

The Woman of Tekoa (for more context, read 2 Samuel 13-14)
c. 2 Samuel 20:

Herodias
c. Matthew 14:1-12:

2) What do you learn about women and their role as "helper" (Genesis 2:18)?

3) How are you challenged by these few examples? Is there something you need to adjust?

Close out the day with prayer and reflection. Record additional insights you discovered that were not addressed in the assignment.

A woman of wisdom and strength is one who arms herself with the Word of God, surrenders her will to the Holy Spirit, and walks in the might of gentleness. She uses her power of persuasion for the glory of God and doesn't war against the call of the Lord on her life with acts of contention but seeks to be at peace with her heavenly Father.

Day 2 – Proverbs 21 – Another View

Something to Consider

"The wicked shall be a ransom for the righteous, and the unfaithful for the upright."

Proverbs 21:18.

RANSOM = To pay the price to release another. To bear the expense or consequence.

Proverbs 21:18 challenged my thinking because my first thought was, how can the wicked be a ransom for the righteous, when the New Testament teaches Jesus is the ransom for humanity?

In the Old Testament, however, it's interesting and worth pausing to look at the meaning of the concept of ransom from another perspective of the same principle, which provides additional clarity into the sovereignty of God.

There are multiple examples of ransom in the book of Exodus, Leviticus and Isaiah that explain the various purposes, which include a foreshadowing of Jesus and his redemptive work on the cross.

Solomon reveals God's hand of justice on the wicked for their actions, individually as well as entire nations, further spotlighting his grace on those who are righteous (in right standing with God through faith). We see evidence of ransom in all 31 chapters, but in chapter 21, Soloman says it plainly.

In addition to the cross-references, today we will read the entire chapter again and note the verses that reflect the wicked earning the wages of their actions, and the righteous being set free. They are a good reminder that tells us ransom is a means of reuniting those who are/ were separated by captivity with another. In our case, Jesus bore the consequence of sin. The price for our freedom was paid with his blood, and death was taken captive instead.

"For the wages of sin is death, but the gift of God is eternal life in Christ Jesus our Lord."

Romans 6:23.

Something to Pray

Father, deepen my understanding of the concept and importance of ransom. May my heart grow in gratitude and trust causing me to surrender in greater ways. Lead me, use me. Be glorified in all I do and say. In the name of Jesus, amen.

Proverbs 21 – Another View

1) Read the following passages and note how they add insight to Proverbs 21:18 and or provide other pictures of ransom.

a. Exodus 21:28-34:

b. Levitus 25:18-50:

c. Isaiah 43:1-4:

d. Romans 5:6-11:

2) Read Proverbs 21 again. Note 3 verses that show evidence of the wicked being a ransom for the righteous.

a.

b.

c.

3) What do you learn about wickedness (sin) and God's justice from the cross references and chapter 21?

4) How are you encouraged to increase your healthy fear of the Lord and decrease your fear of society or others?

5) What is one thing you will stop doing that will reflect your growth in wisdom and what is your plan to implement it?

Proverbs 21 – Closing Thought

"To do righteousness and justice is more acceptable to the LORD than sacrifice."

Proverbs 21:3.

Wisdom's direction is clear. It's a matter of choice to have righteous beliefs, righteous thinking and righteous behavior. Any service, offerings of money or time, have no eternal value apart from walking in the Spirit and a will surrendered in humility and gratitude. Acts of service, while condemnation, criticism, and gossip are present in our lives, place us on the side of wicked behavior. Jesus paid a ransom price for us to be set free from the wages of sin, and the bondage of it. Will we choose to let this truth replace vain sacrifices?

It's our insecurity and fear of others that cause us to act as if we are still in bondage. May we place our misguided fear in the hands of the righteous God, who weighs our hearts and walk in the deliverance he provided on the cross. May we follow righteousness and mercy with a heart of gratitude because when we do, we will find life, righteousness and honor (Proverbs 21:21).

Don't believe the lies of the wicked one who shoots darts that tempt us to wander from the way of understanding and live as though we are dead (Proverbs 21:16).

Live in the perfect love of God. Refuse to settle into the imperfect love of humanity, it only breeds irrational fear and unsettles our soul.

"There is no fear in love; but perfect love cast out fear, because fear involves torment, but he who fears has not been made perfect in love."

1 John 4:18.

The best way to be made perfect in God's perfect love is to lay our will down at the foot of the cross and prepare for the day of battle through prayer and his Word knowing deliverance is in the hands of God. He is the protector of our soul and the avenger of sin. I choose to rest in his redeeming love. How about you?

Related passages: Ruth 4:1-13; Psalm 49:7-8; Isaiah 2:11; Isaiah 35:10; 2 Thessalonians 1:6-8

Close out the day with prayer and reflection. Record additional insights you discovered that were not addressed in the assignment.

Pride keeps us from the position of peace with God that Jesus came to give. This peace is not based on feelings or emotions, or giddiness and goosebumps. The position of peace means we are not at war with our heavenly Father. It's an assurance that brings contentment and calm during a storm. What does it mean to be at war with God? It's a refusal to trust him. It's a decision to trust ourselves and our thoughts and feelings over his truth. It's when our actions show that we believe God is being unjust or holding back on what we think is best. We see pride and foolishness in action throughout the book of Proverbs, and it never ends well. Life, righteousness and honor come when we raise our white flag and end our war against our sovereign Lord.

Day 3 – Proverbs 22

Something to Consider

Proverbs 22 is divided into 3 parts:
- Wise observations using common sense and theological truth
- Wisdom herself speaking to, and questioning her audience
- "Do not" statements and a concluding rhetorical question

It's as if there is a sense that the audience is growing weary in well-doing and needs a reminder from wisdom to wake up and pay attention. A wake-up call to reiterate all that has previously been said as it relates to mind, body and soul:

"Have I not written you excellent things of counsel and knowledge…"
Proverbs 22:20.
"Have I not written for you thirty sayings of counsel and knowledge…"
Proverbs 22:20 (ESV).

The Hebrew word for excellence in the Strong's concordance is Shalish or Shilshom. These words express a gaining of the highest level, and/or have a triple-meaning, expressing fullness, leading a translation of (30). Others simply see it as a literal number of 30. I did a google search. Some have noted 30 specific sayings from Proverbs 22:20 – chapter 24. Indeed, they are excellent and there are 30; however, there are hundreds of sayings, if not thousands that Solomon stated, which are not recorded in the Bible:

"Thus Solomon's wisdom excelled the wisdom of all the men of the East and all the wisdom of Egypt…He spoke three thousand proverbs and his songs were one thousand and five."
1 Kings 4:30,32.

Whether 30 is symbolic or specific to Proverbs 22-24, it's evident that the words of wisdom are most excellent because they provide instructions to live a life of godliness, and more importantly, they represent the character of God.

Something to Pray

Father, above all else, I desire to know and live out your wisdom. As you fill my mind, give me the faith to walk in my commitment to you. In the name of Jesus, amen.

Proverbs 22
The Big Picture

Read Proverbs chapter 22, then answer the following questions.

1) List 3 positive outcomes of wise choices found in verses 1-16. Note the verse in which they were found.

a.

b.

c.

2) List 3 negative outcomes of foolish choices found in verses 1-16. Note the verse in which they were found.

a.

b.

c.

3) List 3 of "sayings of the wise" related to why wisdom is excellent found in verses 17-21. Note the verse and why you chose them.

a.

b.

c.

4) List 3 of the "Do Not" statements found in verses 22-29. Note the verse and why you chose them.

a.

b.

c.

5) What is most encouraging and challenging to you and how will it grow your faith moving forward?

Deeper Reflection

The soul is mentioned three times in Proverbs 22:

"Thorns and snares are in the way of the perverse; he who guards his soul will be far from them."

Proverbs 22:5.

"Do not rob the poor because he is poor, nor oppress the afflicted at the gate; for the LORD will plead their cause, and plunder the soul of those who plunder them."

Proverbs 22:22-23.

"Make no friendship with an angry man, and with a furious man do not go, lest you learn his ways and set a snare for your soul."

Proverbs 22:24-25.

In these three verses we see the responsibility of the righteous and the sovereignty of God in action. The first verse noted tells us that we have a choice and responsibility to guard our soul. The book of Proverbs gives us plenty of practical steps on how we can do this. The two verses that follow reflect a person who is not guarding their soul and the consequence of it. They speak to a lifestyle, and not momentary or sporadic inaction or choices. It's important to recognize this because for some of us over-thinkers and perfectionists, we can scare ourselves into a frenzy.

Under the old covenant, outward behavior and commitment to holiness was dependent on keeping the law and was a matter of the will and godly sense. Under the new, it still involves our will, but it is submission to the Holy Spirit and trusting his grace instead of anything else that can easily trap us into fear-of-man choices.

But what is our soul being guarded from? And how do our faith choices make it possible? Let's spend a little more time exploring these questions.

The use of the word soul and heart are often interchanged because the heart is where beliefs start and directly affect the soul—where feelings, emotions and actions are played out.

"Therefore we also, since we are surrounded by so great a cloud of witnesses, let us lay aside every weight, and the sin which so easily ensnares us, and let us run with endurance the race that is set before us, looking unto Jesus, the author and finisher of our faith, who for the joy that was set before Him endured the cross, despising the shame, and has sat down at the right hand of the throne of God."

Hebrews 12:1-2.

1) Read through Proverbs 22 again. Note 3 verses that give an example of how we can guard our soul. What is the subtle or obvious faith choice involved, and what might it cost?

a.

b.

c.

2) Read the following passages and note what they say about faith choices that guard our soul/heart?

a. Joshua 23:11-16:

b. Psalm 91:1-16:

c. 1 Peter 5:6-9:

3) What do you conclude about what and who is at the center of guarding your soul and what will you do this week to make a faith choice that God's Word has prompted you to make?

Close out the day with prayer and reflection. Record additional insights you discovered that were not addressed in the assignment.

"In my distress I cried to the LORD and He heard me. Deliver my soul, O LORD from lying lips and from a deceitful tongue."

Psalm 120:1-2.

Day 4 – Another View

Something to Consider

We live in a time of a great falling away from accountability and discipline, primarily in the home. This leads to a society of entitlement and lack of respect for parents and the law. Unfortunately, it's not much different in the church where many give an incomplete expression and extension of God's love.

The fullness of God's love includes accountability, discipline and consequence, and because of this, the Holy Spirit will convict our hearts. As one of God's attributes, he instructs parents to do the same with their children so they can grow into wise and healthy adults.

Looking back a few verses, we can see a path laid out for us that speaks to accountability and correction:

"Thorns and snares are in the way of the perverse; he who guards his soul will be far from them." Therefore, it would be wise to, "Train up a child in the way he should go, and when he is old he will not depart from it." Because, "Foolishness is bound up in the heart of a child; The rod of correction will drive it far from him."

Proverbs 22:5-6, 15.

There is no shortage of evidence for lack of physical and spiritual discipline in the disturbing and painful events that take place daily. The temptation is to judge the person with contempt instead of their behavior. We can easily forget that our fight is not against flesh and blood, but against the spiritual hosts of wickedness. We should first ask, what is the person lacking that caused such behavior, so that our hearts turn to prayer without condemning the person because God is the only one who knows the whole story.

Today we will focus on spiritual discipline and why it's so important for us to stay humble and teachable as children of God, because we too can have foolishness bound up in our hearts.

Something to Pray

Heavenly Father, help me to nurture others and encourage them in your ways and their gifts instead of my own. Humble the areas of my heart where I have forgotten I am your child and that I don't always have it altogether. Teach me. In the name of Jesus, amen.

Proverbs 22 – Another View

1) Read the following passages and note how they add insight to Proverbs 22:15.

a. Deuteronomy 8:5-6:

b. 2 Timothy 3:16-17:

c. Hebrews 12:5-11:

2) What comes to mind when you think about discipline, and how do your life experiences affect your thinking?

3) Do you know someone who may lack discipline? How can you use wisdom to address this with kindness?

4) How are you challenged by Proverbs 22?

Proverbs 22 – Closing Thought

Proverbs 22 touches on all aspects of life; finances, discipline, laziness, emotions and generosity to name a few. Each should be addressed with wisdom and humility.

When we maintain a teachable spirit, we will be able to readily receive clear vision and instruction, and though we may trip and stumble, we will not fall blindly into the devil's deep pit of quicksand. Remember the immoral woman's goal is to seduce us in our weaknesses and lack of knowledge. Let's not willingly make her job easy.

"Beloved, I pray that you may prosper in all things and be in health, just as your soul prospers. For I rejoiced greatly when brethren came and testified of the truth that is in you, just as you walk in the truth. I have no greater joy than to hear that my children walk in truth."
3 John 1:2-4.

"...that their hearts may be encouraged, being knit together in love, and attaining to all riches of the full assurance of understanding, to the knowledge of the mystery of God, both of the Father and of Christ, in whom are hidden all the treasures of wisdom and knowledge."
Colossians 2:2-3.

Let's be women who prosper in the riches and honor of Christ Jesus our Lord by pursuing a good name rather than the corruptible riches of this world. Let's be women who stay away from senseless conflict and scoffers and rest in the absence of strife. Let's be women who do not fear others and their weapons, but remember God is our strength.

Related passages: Romans 12:17-18; 16:17; Titus 3:9

Close out the day with prayer and reflection. Record additional insights you discovered that were not addressed in the assignment.

"The LORD preserves those with knowledge, but he ruins the plans of the treacherous. A lazy person says, 'There's a lion out there! If I go outside, I might be killed!'"

Proverbs 22:12-13 (NLT).

The slothful man always finds reasons for not stepping out. The slothful man will stay inside and miss the opportunity to move out for God, failing to understand that while our enemy is indeed a lion (1 Peter 5:8), we have within us the power of the Lion of the tribe of Judah (Revelation 5:5). It was fear of the enemy that kept the Israelites out of the Promised Land (Numbers 12:32,33). But they eventually entered the Land, only to discover that, all along, their enemies were afraid of them and their God (Joshua 2:9-11). Oh, if we only realized that, truly, greater is He that is within us than he that is in the world. (1 John 4:4).
– Jon Courson

Day 5 – Proverbs 23

Something to Consider

Most of the warnings in chapter 23 are related to our inner belief and intents of the heart.

We are challenged to examine the people and situations placed before us, most notably eating and drinking. These are reminiscent of the New Testament teachings of Jesus and the apostles. When we use wisdom, we will spare ourselves heartache.

The key to preservation is found midway through the chapter:

"Don't envy sinners, but always continue to fear the LORD. You will be rewarded for this; your hope will not be disappointed."
Proverbs 23:17-18 (NLT).

When we have envy in our hearts or are impressed with worldly riches and status, our sight and decision-making can get blurry and we end up in a tough situation, or as stated in 4 chapters: "In the end"...

Eating and drinking are directly connected to relationships and celebrations and are wonderful gifts from God. The difference is with whom we are eating and what we are drinking as Solomon mentions in the first verse. He uses the metaphorical phrase put a knife to your throat, which comes with the idea of self-control and discipline.

"While dining with a ruler, pay attention to what is put before you. If you are a big eater, put a knife to your throat: don't desire all the delicacies, for he might be trying to trick you."
Proverbs 23:1-3 (NLT).

As you read through this chapter, consider the strong connection to relationships, with others and with behaviors. We are created for interaction. What kind and with whom will we pursue?

Something to Pray

Heavenly Father, I ask for your help to pay attention to what is before me and give me the courage to pursue the eating and drinking of your Word above all else. May wisdom lead me as I bend my will to yours. In the name of Jesus, amen.

Proverbs 23
The Big Picture

Read chapter 23, then answer the following questions.

1) List 3 things you learn about the heart: positive and negative. Note the verse and how you see belief in action/behavior.

a.

b.

c.

2) List 2 things you learn about relationships and the characteristics of humanity. Note the verse in which you found them and why you chose them.

a.

b.

3) What senses does the appeal of alcohol call out to in verse 31? How could this apply to any other destructive behavior?

4) What do you see as the tipping point in the decision to be swayed by the harlot/immoral woman?

5) Which of the behaviors mentioned in this chapter challenges you and what have you learned about it that can change your heart in the matter?

6) What is one thing you will do to strengthen your faith this week?

Deeper Reflection

The following two statements have an especially strong significance for the Jewish people:

"When you sit down to eat with a ruler, consider carefully what is before you."

Proverbs 23:1.

"Do not remove the ancient landmark, nor enter the fields of the fatherless; For their Redeemer is mighty; He will plead their cause against you."

Proverbs 23:10-11.

There are several examples in the Old Testament of kings holding elaborate banquets for the sole purpose of manipulation and striking deals. Often invited were lessor rulers of smaller provinces and statuses that were thrilled to be included and already in a vulnerable position.

Secondly, God was very specific about territories allotted to each tribe, and gave instructions on management, protection and the people within those territories as well as warned of the wicked kings and kingdoms that surrounded them. To fall in one of these two areas, or both, would be evidence of how far from God and wisdom one had become, and all the consequences that would follow.

The warning here is to exercise sound judgment through godly wisdom and not put themselves in a position to be pressured or manipulated. I am reminded of Proverbs 5:6 which says the lips of the immoral woman drip with honey and her mouth is smoother than oil. We don't want to consider her path at all because the way of evil is unstable, and we can't possibly know the depth of its schemes to destroy.

Let's spend a little bit more time looking at these two concepts and the boundaries set by God that are designed to protect us. It is good for us to remember the early statements from Solomon regarding wisdom as we continue through the proverbs that lay out practical choices related to life and staying on the right path.

"When wisdom enters your heart and knowledge is pleasant to your soul, discretion will preserve you; understanding will keep you, to deliver you from the way of evil. From the man who speaks perverse things, from those who leave the paths of uprightness to walk in the ways of darkness."

Proverbs 2:10-13.

1) Read the following passages and note how they add insight to Proverbs 23:1 and 23:10-11. Also note how you see manipulation/plotting in play and the outcome.

a. Daniel 3:1-25:

b. Daniel 6:1-23:

c. Acts 6:7-12, 7:51-8:3:

2) How do you see wisdom used in the three stories in question 1? What gave them courage to consider what was before them and choose the straight path?

3) How did wisdom preserve Stephen from evil?

4) How do these stories challenge you to consider what is before you and choose the way of wisdom regardless of the cost?

Close out the day with prayer and reflection. Record additional insights you discovered that were not addressed in the assignment.

"Don't be afraid of those who want to kill your body; they cannot touch your soul. Fear only God, who can destroy both soul and body in hell."
Matthew 10:28.

Day 6 – Proverbs 23 – Another View

Something to Consider

Solomon touches on eating and drinking in the early part of the chapter, but spends a good portion toward the end warning of drinking in greater detail. Throughout this chapter we can see the beginning of compromise and where it leads.

This chapter provides a good example of Psalm 1 in action: Walk. Stand. Sit. Let's get a fresh look at the progression:

"Blessed is the man who walks not in the counsel of the ungodly, nor stands in the path of sinners, nor sits in the seat of the scornful."

Psalm 1:1.

The first step of compromise is walking in (listening) to ungodly counsel. It applies to their philosophy in every aspect of life. It can desensitize us if we walk in it too long. The second step is to stop and listen, which implies resting in it with greater interest. The pull gains strength the longer we stand, and we land in a place where we sit and participate.

A harmless picture of this could be a street musician or artist. I've done this countless times at amusement parks. Can you think of a time when music caught your ear either on route to something important or just strolling through the park? What did you do?

Though alcohol is the example in chapter 23, this same road to destruction can be applied to many other addictive and compulsive behaviors. I recognize this may be an uncomfortable and painful subject for many, and with this, I pause to encourage you to reach out if you need support in allowing God to heal you.

Choosing to face pain is a wise decision and requires trusting God with our will in greater ways.

Today we will focus on what we can do to avoid the pitfalls of compromise.

Something to Pray

Heavenly Father, I pray for my own areas of need for healing as well as all your children. Help us to be a source of encouragement to one another and promote wellness instead of pain. In the name of Jesus, amen.

Proverbs 23 – Another View

1) Read Proverbs 23. Note the passages you see that lay out the steps of compromise related to alcohol, and the warning given.

2) Write out other scenarios this can apply to in our lives.

3) What is an area of weakness for you? From chocolate to shopping to severely destructive behaviors—what do you learn from Proverbs 23 regarding compromise?

4) Look up the following passages, note the solution they provide to compromise.

a. Proverbs 4:14-15:

b. Romans 13:13-14:

c. Ephesians 5:1-7:

5) What is one area that you have been complacent in that has compromised you or is in danger of your compromise, and what is your plan to change it?

Proverbs 23 – Closing Thought

"Don't envy sinners, But always continue to fear the LORD."

Proverbs 23:17 (NLT).

"Get the truth and never sell it; also get wisdom, discipline, and good judgment."

Proverbs 23:23 (NLT).

"For the harlot is a deep pit, and a seductress is a narrow well. She also lies in wait as for a victim and increases the unfaithful among men."

Proverbs 23:27-28.

The verses referenced above call to mind the earlier chapters that are heavy with encouragement and warning to keep wisdom as a treasure and to stay far away from the path of the immoral woman. I can't help but think they are small but powerful reminders inserted into sections that are ripe with sinful behavior because of rejecting wisdom. It's not known how closely the original conversation of each letter happened or written down, organized and dispersed, so it's only a guess as to the shift in intensity from warning to examples as we have seen happen throughout what has become known as the Book of Proverbs.

It's not important to know how they were previously distributed, though it is important for us to take full advantage of the gift of having them all neatly brought together by the Holy Spirit. This is what came to my mind, I pray it serves as an encouragement to keep digging and not grow weary of the constant reminders and similar topics we have studied through this chapter, and will no doubt touch on moving forward.

Take a moment to consider all you have learned from God's Word. Thank him for his faithfulness to reveal himself to you in greater ways as you listen to wisdom as she raises her voice (Prov 1:20). She is faithful to give us clear vision. Yes, clear vision, indeed.

Related passages: Proverbs 3:5-6; Matthew 7:13-14; John 14:6; 1 Peter 5:8

Close out the day with prayer and reflection. Record additional insights you discovered that were not addressed in the assignment.

"Blessed is the man who walks not in the counsel of the ungodly, nor stands in the path of sinners, nor sits in the seat of the scornful; But his delight is in the law of the LORD, and in His law he meditates day and night. He shall be like a tree planted by the rivers of water, that brings forth its fruit in its season, whose leaf also shall not wither; and whatever he does shall prosper. The ungodly are not so, but are like the chaff which the wind drives away. Therefore the ungodly shall not stand in the judgment, nor sinners in the congregation of the righteous. For the LORD knows the way of the righteous, but the way of the ungodly shall perish."
Psalm 1.

Day 7

Reflect on this week's assignments and note any additional thoughts below. For group studies, choose 1 or 2 questions from each day and discuss as a group and record your thoughts and/or prayer requests.

Week Three

She GIVES Strength

Proverbs 24-25

Day 1 - Proverbs 24

Something to Consider

Proverbs 24 has two overarching contrasts: healthy relationships through wisdom and unhealthy relationships through foolishness. Each offers a host of rewards and consequences, not much different from previous chapters with one exception: strength, rather than emotion, is a factor in rising or falling.

Strength in wisdom is what gives us the ability to withstand temptation, accusation and mistreatment. Full strength comes from aligning our will with God's truth regardless of how we feel or what we think. It comes from our core belief in God's character rather than our personal experiences.

Daily and life-changing matters are directly affected by the amount of godly wisdom and godly relationships we have in our lives, and the choices we make will act as evidence to the degree in which we have grown.4

Some of the themes covered are:
- Jealousy and envy
- How to build a healthy home
- How to fight the good fight of faith
- How to discern good and evil/ healthy and unhealthy
- How to learn from the lessons of others
- Don't celebrate the fall of an enemy

We could sum it up and say Proverbs 24 is about relationships, and while true, there are too many details for us to see and learn how to apply along the way to be satisfied with that.

Resist a quick or glossed over read-through of this chapter because of its familiar message. Pause at the end of each statement to consider its message. What is God's Word asking of you?

Something to Pray

Father, I confess there is no excuse for my weak areas, except that I have grown weary of well-doing and can get comfortable with "well enough" at times. Thank you for filling me with strength as I diligently seek the wisdom found in your truth. Help me to learn from those who have gone before me. In the name of Jesus, amen.

Proverbs 24
The Big Picture

Read Proverbs chapter 24, then answer the following questions.

1) What is the first thing Solomon says not to do, and what effect on strength can it have if we do?

2) List all that you learn about how a house is built and what does this mean for you in this season of your life?

3) What is the evidence that strength is small/weak? How does this challenge you?

4)What do you learn about the "righteous/godly"? List all the verses that you find.

5) How are you encouraged and challenged toward your relationships—family and friends?

Deeper Reflection

"The godly may trip seven times, but they will get up again, but one disaster is enough to overthrow the wicked."
Proverbs 24:16.

Persistence. Endurance. Perseverance. These traits are a sign of hard work and diligence. There isn't a lot of pomp and circumstance like the sparkling traits of the wicked one, but they build a solid foundation for success. The glory is seen in the outcome, not necessarily the pursuit. The pursuit can get a bit messy and one can acquire a few bumps and bruises along the way.

The first time I went roller skating, I was hooked. I wasn't into the traditional and more popular sports, but roller skating changed everything. My sister and I lived for it. Any chance we had we took it. It was my goal to learn how to skate backwards and sideways and do all the fancy tricks everyone else was doing. I skated faster and harder each time, falling more often and harder in the process. After a while, I was an advanced backward and side skater, and had a blast at speedskating and roller derby. It wasn't any fun falling. It was painful and embarrassing, but I didn't care. My eye was on the goal. Quitting wasn't an option. Not even when others would tell me I was never going to get it. Instead of caving to humiliation and being laughed at, stubborn determination won out. What about you? What drives you?

"Do not rejoice over me my enemy; When I fall, I will arise; When I sit in darkness, the LORD will be a light to me."
Micah 7:8.

The older I get, the more that passage means to me. It's the verse for Rise Up, the ministry for women seeking healing and freedom from trauma. It was a powerful word for the Israelites when they were coming out of captivity and being trampled by their enemies. It's also a powerful word of truth for today for all of us who are learning to stand in the grace and knowledge of God. The enemy seeks our demise and wants us to live in discouragement, and if we are weak, he will succeed.

"If you faint in the day of adversity, your strength is small."
Proverbs 24:10.

Let's spend a little bit more time looking at passages that challenge us to strengthen our resolve through wise choices.

1) Read the following passages. Note how they add insight to Proverbs 24:10.

a. John 8:31-32:

b. John 16:33:

c. Ephesians 4:14-24:

2) What would some of your choices, past or present, say about your strength in Christ?

3) Is there something concerning you today that the enemy could be using to tempt you to turn from God and move to something or someone seemingly safer and more comforting?

4) What is one thing you can do to grow in strength moving forward?

Close out the day with prayer and reflection. Record additional insights you discovered that were not addressed in the assignment.

"Therefore gird up the loins of your mind, be sober, and rest your hope fully upon the grace that is to be brought to you at the revelation of Jesus Christ."

1 Peter 1:13.

Day 2 – Proverbs 24 – Another View

Something to Consider

"I walked by the field of a lazy person, and the vineyard of one with no common sense. I saw that it was overgrown with nettles. It was covered with weeds, and its walls were broken down. Then, as I looked and thought about it, I learned this lesson: A little extra sleep, a little more slumber, a little folding of the hands to rest— then poverty will pounce on you like a bandit; scarcity will attack you like an armed robber."

Proverbs 24:30-34.

Proverbs 24:30-34 give a visual picture of what can happen when we get complacent and lazy. What we see externally, is something that began internally. Hardships in life can have a direct effect on the beliefs of our heart and change our thinking and behavior.

Have you ever put something off because you just didn't want to think about it? Procrastination and reluctance are a sister to laziness, and they all lead to neglect.

This principle of laziness in outward work applies to our spiritual walk. The Bible instructs us to tend to our faith so that we can withstand in the difficult times and avoid a chaotic tangled mess of weeds.

"Finally, my brethren, be strong in the Lord and in the power of His might. Put on the whole armor of God, that you may be able to stand against the wiles of the devil."

Ephesians 6:10-11.

Today we will focus on passages that speak to the importance of tending to our faith. We should never be comfortable with well-enough or settle into thinking we are better than we were before, so there is no need to pursue grace and knowledge in deeper ways.

Something to Pray

Father, convict my heart of areas that I have settled into laziness or procrastination in seeking you with a fervent mind and heart. Help me to see where weeds have grown so that I will allow you to pluck them out by their roots and bring order into all the areas of my life. Help me to be a source of encouragement to others in the process. In the name of Jesus, amen.

Proverbs 24 – Another View

1) Read the following passages and note how they add insight to Proverbs 24:30-34 on a spiritual level.

a. Hebrews 1:1-2:4:

b. Hebrews 6:10-12:

c. 1 Peter 3:15:

2) Is there an area of your walk of faith that you have grown into complacency and laziness? If so, note it, and pause to confess it.

3) What passage above challenges you most and what is your plan to surrender your will in greater ways to Jesus today?

Proverbs 24 – Closing Thought

A house is built by wisdom and becomes strong through good sense. Through knowledge its rooms are filled with all sorts of precious riches and valuables."

Proverbs 24:1-4 (NLT).

Warmth in a home is not measured by the style of furnishings, the one-of-a-kind piece of art, or exquisite landscape. These all fade with time and do not add value to our life. There is nothing wrong with having these things, but they should never be our pursuit or where we find our value and identity because it can be lost at any time.

The riches and valuables wisdom provides are lasting peace, contentment and joy. No matter what our station in life, goodness and mercy are present and all who enter our home will experience the warm presence. This is a worthy and lasting pursuit. May we all choose it over status or the temptation to envy what others have.

It's been said, "The grass may be greener on the other side of the fence, but it could be due to a sewage leak." This saying comes to mind when I find myself getting a bit jealous of someone who has something I want.

Proverbs 24 offers many strategies for finding freedom from the pressures of this world. It would be wise for us to pursue them without growing weary in well-doing (Galatians 6:9) and choose to walk in the strength wisdom provides.

"And He said to me, "My grace is sufficient for you, for My strength is made perfect in weakness." Therefore most gladly I will rather boast in my infirmities, that the power of Christ may rest upon me. Therefore I take pleasure in infirmities, in reproaches, in needs, in persecutions, in distresses, for Christ's sake. For when I am weak, then I am strong."

2 Corinthians 12:9-10.

Related passages: Romans 10:17; Colossians 2:6-7; Hebrews 10:23

Close out the day with prayer and reflection. Record additional insights you discovered that were not addressed in the assignment.

"How sweet are Your words to my taste, Sweeter than honey to my mouth! Through Your precepts I get understanding; Therefore I hate every false way."

Psalm 119:103-104.

Day 3 – Proverbs 25

Something to Consider

Every statement written speaks of the effect we can have on others. It boils down to two options; wound or comfort. Chapters 1-24 provide a wide range of examples of how our beliefs and will (wickedness or wisdom) affect our behavior toward others.

The style of this chapter differs from many others in that each verse is a short, but practical picture of individual thoughts instead of a longer narrative. They are simple and do not require deep contemplation, however, these Solomon-isms, cut deep into our hearts, minds and souls with a challenge to choose wisely.

Jesus, James, and Paul quoted many of these sayings word for word or taught the same principle using similar examples which serve as beautiful reminders that God's character never changes.

His agape (unconditional) love toward us should compel us to let that love flow through us and transform us into the image of Christ. It is the only way that we can surrender our will to his in greater ways.

Our thoughts, feelings and behaviors should be in alignment with God's will for all his children, but the truth is, this isn't always the case. And when it's not, we need to be obedient to love and encourage others even if we don't "feel" like it. When we serve one another in sacrifice as a love offering from Christ, our feelings will change, and even if there isn't an immediate shift, our hearts will respond. When our heart changes, our thoughts follow, and inevitably our feelings will change as well.

It's helpful to keep the power of our will in mind as we study this chapter a little further.

Something to Pray

Heavenly Father, when my feelings overwhelm me, help me to choose your will over my own. Humble me to set my will aside and consider your grace in my life so I will choose to pass it on to those around me and not wallow in my feelings. More of you, less of me. Thank you for such practical advice. I have no excuse to say I don't know what you want of me. In the name of Jesus, amen.

Proverbs 25
The Big Picture

1) What do you learn about God's character in this chapter?

2) What is your understanding of verse 4 and how do you see this active in your life?

3) List 3 statements that challenge your thinking and behavior. Note the verse and the challenge put before you.

a.

b.

c.

4) What is one example in this season of your life where your heart, mind and soul are not in alignment with one another in what God's will is for how we treat others?

5) What is it that you need to get them in alignment?

Deeper Reflection

"Like a city that is broken into and without walls is a man who has no control over his spirit."

Proverbs 25:28 (NASB).

Solomon uses a city without walls as a strong comparison to those who lack self-control. It is the perfect analogy because the Jewish people understood the high importance God set on walls/boundaries to warn and protect. In the Old and New Testament walls/boundaries, including gates, serve as physical and spiritual advisors and protectors. They are designed to warn us and remind us to prepare for battle before the enemy's attack. Without walls or boundaries, the enemy is free to wander unnoticed until it's too late.

Let's take a little more time to look at a few examples of walls and boundaries in the Bible that God placed in creation and for his children.

1) Read the following passages and note the practical application you can pull from each.

a. Nehemiah 9:22:

b. 2 Corinthians 6:14-18:

c. Galatians 5:16-26:

2) How would you rate your spiritual boundaries and walls of protection? Note 1 physical and 1 spiritual that are challenging for you and rate it between 1-5. How do they relate to your ability to have self-control?

a.

b.

Close out the day with prayer and reflection. Record additional insights you discovered that were not addressed in the assignment.

Healthy and godly boundaries are important to our spiritual growth and are evidence that we are walking in wisdom.

"Do not get involved in foolish discussions about spiritual pedigrees or in quarrels and fights about obedience to Jewish laws. These things are useless and a waste of time. If people are causing divisions among you, give a first and second warning. After that, have nothing more to do with them. For people like that have turned away from the truth, and their own sins condemn them."

Titus 3:9-10 (NLT).

Day 4 – Proverbs 25 – Another View

Something to Consider

When my husband and I married we were not believers. Roughly two years in, God began to tug at my heart, reminding me of a half-hearted reciting of the sinner's prayer I muttered when I was 17. This tugging came while driving home after hearing our baby's heartbeat for the first time, 12-ish weeks into my pregnancy. By the time I arrived home, the tears were flowing. The fountains of my hardened heart, stubborn mind, and tough exterior erupted into uncontrollable sobs as I fell to my knees at the realization of the choices I made at 16 and 17 years old. They weren't just blobs of tissue as I desperately needed to believe, they were babies.

That January day in 1988 was the day I surrendered my life to Christ and stopped fighting him. I was humbled to my core as a wave of repentance and freedom washed over me. I vowed never to go back to that stubborn, say-what-I-think, no filter girl. She was dead.

I am being gracious when I say that it lasted two weeks. I grew tired of being a sappy girl who cried when a petal fell off a rose. That is no way for strong women to live. It was much safer to keep the upper hand.

About 3 years into my walk with God, I had just enough knowledge to be dangerous coupled with the fact that grace was still a concept I didn't fully grasp. Yet in his grace, God had given me opportunities to teach. It was clear that teaching was his calling on my life. Little did I know, the teacher had much to learn.

Humble pie. Worst taste ever.

I lost count of how many times I was knocked off my high-horse, or how many sledgehammers God had to use to break my hardened heart and wall built with my pride. I was convicted about my piercing words and the sharp darts from my eyes that served to keep me safe for so long.

It's easy for us to forget where we came from, especially if that was a healthy environment, with not much "big sin" to speak of. It's even easier to think we come to a place where we are pretty good and have been elevated in status with God. Wrong. Today we will look at several passages that have a lot to say about humility with Proverbs 25:6-7 in mind.

Something to Pray

Father, humble me in the areas that are still full of pride. Help me graciously take the back seat and let others sit in front in every situation. In the name of Jesus, amen.

Proverbs 25 – Another View

"Do not exalt yourself in the presence of the king, And do not stand in the place of the great; For it is better that he say to you, "Come up here," than that you should be put lower in the presence of the prince, whom your eyes have seen."

Proverbs 25:6-7.

1) Read the following passages and note how they add insight to Proverbs 25:6-7.

a. 1 Samuel 2:3:

b. Philippians 2:1-8:

c. James 4:13-16:

2) Is there an area where pride is active in your life? How is it affecting you and your relationships?

3) What is one thing you will do to lay your pride down at the feet of Jesus? What is it going to cost you?

4) What do you learn about the heart of Jesus from Philippians 4:1-8, and how does it encourage you to live out the principles in Proverbs 25?

Proverbs 25 – Closing Thought

If we are unable to submit our will to the will of God and trust him in greater ways for the courage and strength it takes to live as he calls us, it will be impossible to humble ourselves to others who challenge our pride.

What will it take for us to push past our comfort zone of where we are today in our walk with God? Does your faith look the same today as it did a year ago? What is the evidence of growth—not in service, but in humility?

Proverbs 25 can also be equated to "The Golden Rule".

"Therefore, whatever you want men to do to you, do also to them, for this is the Law and the Prophets."

Matthew 7:12.

"Put on then, as God's chosen ones, holy and beloved, compassionate hearts, kindness, humility, meekness, and patience, bearing with one another and, if one has a complaint against another, forgiving each other; as the Lord has forgiven you, so you also must forgive."

Colossians 3:12-13 (ESV).

"Finally, all of you, have unity of mind, sympathy, brotherly love, a tender heart, and a humble mind. Do not repay evil for evil or reviling for reviling, but on the contrary, bless, for to this you were called, that you may obtain a blessing."

1 Peter 3:8-9 (ESV).

My thoughts go back to the earlier chapters of Proverbs. Particularly, Proverbs 3:1-4, which instructs us to keep kindness and truth around our neck and written on our hearts. I am challenged to consider how well I have done that throughout this study of Proverbs. What has changed in me? How about you?

Related passages: Zechariah 7:9-10; Romans 12:10; Galatians 6:2-9

Close out the day with prayer and reflection. Record additional insights you discovered that were not addressed in the assignment.

"He has shown you, O man, what is good; And what does the LORD require of you but to do justly, to love mercy, and to walk humbly with your God?"
Micah 6:8.

Day 5 – Proverbs 25 – Continued

Something to Consider

On day three, I shared that Proverbs 25 has multiple quotes and principles shared by Jesus, James and Paul in the New Testament.

Today will be a day of searching out passages for yourself that reflect these Proverbs 25 principles. Some may have already come to mind, and others are yet to be discovered.

You can use google searches using the phrases in the verses, or a concordance for similar themes.

This exercise is a practical way to put earlier instructions into practice:

"My son, if you receive my words, and treasure my commands within you, so that you incline your ear to wisdom, and apply your heart to understanding; Yes, if you cry out for discernment, and lift up your voice for understanding, If you seek her as silver, and search for her as for hidden treasures; Then you will understand the fear of the LORD, and find the knowledge of God. For the LORD gives wisdom; From His mouth come knowledge and understanding; He stores up sound wisdom for the upright; He is a shield to those who walk uprightly."
Proverbs 2: 1-7.

"Get wisdom! Get understanding! Do not forget, nor turn away from the words of my mouth. Do not forsake her, and she will preserve you; Love her, and she will keep you. Wisdom is the principal thing; Therefore get wisdom. And in all your getting, get understanding. Exalt her, and she will promote you; She will bring you honor, when you embrace her. She will place on your head an ornament of grace; A crown of glory she will deliver to you."
Proverbs 4:5-9.

Something to Pray

Father, stretch my knowledge of your Word. Give me understanding and fill my heart with another layer of grace and love and trust for you that will be evident to those around me. In the name of Jesus, amen.

Read Proverbs 25. Note 5 verses that pique your interest, then look up the New Testament quote or equivalent principle, and where you found them. Note any additional insights you gain.

1)

2)

3)

4)

5)

6) What drew your attention to the 5 you chose? How do you see them active in your life today and what encourages you that you are growing in wisdom and knowledge? What is the evidence?

Close out the day with prayer and reflection. Record additional insights you discovered that were not addressed in the assignment.

"How can a young man cleanse his way? By taking heed according to Your word. With my whole heart I have sought You; Oh, let me not wander from Your commandments! Your word I have hidden in my heart, that I might not sin against You. Blessed are You, O LORD! Teach me Your statutes. With my lips I have declared all the judgments of Your mouth. I have rejoiced in the way of Your testimonies, as much as in all riches. I will meditate on Your precepts, and contemplate Your ways. I will delight myself in Your statutes; I will not forget Your word."

Psalm 119:9–16.

Day 6 – Reflections

Something to Consider

It's a good idea to stop and look back to the beginning to see how far we've come and to examine our faith. Are we growing? Are we stagnant and just going through the emotions, or have we gotten off track completely?

The truth is, even when we are going to church, attending Bible studies and serving on a regular basis, stagnation or turning to the left or right (Proverbs 4:27) is possible. If not, we wouldn't have reminders throughout the Bible to keep ourselves in check.

"Let us search out and examine our ways, and turn back to the Lord."
Lamentations 3:40.

"Examine yourselves as to whether you are in the faith. Test yourselves. Do you not know yourselves, that Jesus Christ is in you?—unless indeed you are disqualified."
2 Corinthians 13:5.

"Test all things; hold fast what is good."
1 Thessalonians 5:21.

Today is a good day to examine ourselves and see how we have grown from studying Proverbs, and some of the principles that may have already taken a back seat to our current situation. If you haven't had an opportunity to complete all sections of the study, this is also a good time to go back and do one or two of them. Whichever the case, use today to reflect on how you have grown in the grace and knowledge of our Lord and Savior Jesus Christ (2 Peter 3:18).

Something to Pray

Father, I praise you and thank you for the ways I have grown and how you have healed me and are doing a work to transform me into the image of Christ. Help me to accept your invitation and challenge to get up and keep moving or to get back on the straight and narrow path. You are an awesome and mighty God, and I give you glory and honor to the degree that I know how. I look forward to how that will continue to grow. In the name of Jesus, amen.

Proverbs – Reflections

Choose up to 4 of the weeks in Part 1 (Proverbs 1-17) or Part 2 (Proverbs 18-31) through this week. From the weeks chosen, pick up to 4 questions and the cross references from them. Note how you have grown since your original answers. Would you answer differently and if so, in what way/s? Note the chapter and verse and why you chose them as well as any new insights gained as of today.

1) Week _____ Proverbs chapter _____ Question _____

a. Original insight:

b. Today's insight:

2) Week _____ Proverbs chapter _____ Question _____

a. Original insight:

b. Today's insight:

3) Week _____ Proverbs chapter _____ Question _____

a. Original insight:

b. Today's insight:

4) Week _____ Proverbs chapter _____ Question _____

a. Original insight:

b. Today's insight:

5) What did you learn about yourself from this exercise?

6) What is 1 praise for growth, and 1 prayer for moving forward?

Close out the day with prayer and reflection. Record additional insights you discovered that were not addressed in the assignment.

"Finally, brethren, whatever things are true, whatever things are noble, whatever things are just, whatever things are pure, whatever things are lovely, whatever things are of good report, if there is any virtue and if there is anything praiseworthy—meditate on these things. The things which you learned and received and heard and saw in me, these do, and the God of peace will be with you."

Philippians 4:8-9.

Day 7

Reflect on this week's assignments and note any additional thoughts below. For group studies, choose 1 or 2 questions from each day and discuss as a group and record your thoughts and/or prayer requests.

Week Four

She GIVES A Way of ESCAPE

Proverbs 26-28

Day 1 – Proverbs 26

Something to Consider

Proverbs 26 is one of the few chapters in the book of Proverbs that does not mention the Lord, wisdom or the immoral woman.

Perhaps it's because the spotlight is on foolish and lazy people. In earlier chapters we learn that a fool is one who has continually rejected the Lord's offering of wisdom for a spiritually prosperous life and ends up living a life of destruction to self and others.

What we see in this chapter are a series of comparisons that expose the character of a foolish person. It speaks of hopelessness that comes with continual rejection but also warns the wise to pay attention and not to form relationships with them. The New Testament takes that thought further and warns believers to part ways with other believers who are knowingly and willfully living in their sin.

It's important to recognize that the warnings do not instruct us to condemn the foolish—believer or not. We separate ourselves because we can easily get drawn in. As we discussed in the previous chapter, spiritual boundaries are important to keep us on the straight path. Equally important is that as we read, if or when some of the statements remind us of someone we know, we need to be sure our thoughts don't turn to judgment—especially if a painful memory comes at us in full-force. If this should happen, it's an indicator that the wound or wounds are not healed. This would be a good time to stop and lay that thought down at the feet of Jesus and ask God to give you the ability to forgive so that you can be healed. Remember, forgiveness does not always include reconciliation. Wisdom helps us discern safe people from unsafe people.

Something to Pray

Heavenly Father, keep me in a place of humility as you call me to stay true to you. Give me a heart of compassion for those who are struggling and turn my thoughts toward prayer. In the name of Jesus, amen.

Proverbs 26
The Big Picture

Read Proverbs chapter 26, then answer the following questions.

1) List 2 pitfalls from the behaviors mentioned in this chapter that can bring down Christ followers if they keep regular company with a foolish person or crowd.

a.

b.

2) List 3 topics mentioned that are found in earlier chapters. Note why you chose them and how your understanding and application has changed since Proverbs 1.

a.

b.

c.

3) Each of these statements express the idea of a waste of valuable time or beating your head against a wall. Which one challenges you most and why?

Deeper Reflection

"Don't answer the foolish arguments of fools, or you will become just as foolish as they are. Be sure to answer the foolish arguments of fools, or they will become wise in their own eyes."

Proverbs 26:4-5.

A surface reading of verses 24-25 shows them to be contradictory. Which is it, we ask? This is one of those passages that people can use to say the Bible is unreliable because it contradicts itself. Nothing could be further from the truth.

The enemy can use these to trip us up by causing us to get confused and frustrated. Wisdom has taught us to think before we speak and examine our heart before getting frustrated. These verses give us the opportunity to pause and consider what is being said because both statements are valid and speak to the idea that there is a right time for everything.

"For everything there is a season, a time for every activity under heaven. A time to be born and a time to die. A time to plant and a time to harvest. A time to kill and a time to heal. A time to tear down and a time to build up. A time to cry and a time to laugh. A time to grieve and a time to dance. A time to scatter stones and a time to gather stones. A time to embrace and a time to turn away. A time to search and a time to quit searching. A time to keep and a time to throw away. A time to tear and a time to mend. A time to be quiet and a time to speak. A time to love and a time to hate. A time for war and a time for peace."

Ecclesiastes 3:1-8 (NLT).

Anytime you read the Bible, and something seems contradictory, pause and apply wise thinking to search out the answer in other parts of Scripture. Today, we will spend a little more time looking at passages that use this principle of when to speak and when to keep silent.

1) Read the following passages. Note how they add insight to Proverbs 26:4-5 and what circumstance could have led to the decision to speak or hold their tongue.

a. Jeremiah chapter 28:

b. Matthew 23:1-15:

c. Matthew 26:57-66:

2) What do you learn about yourself regarding speaking up and remaining silent? What is your motive?

3) What will you do differently going forward?

Close out the day with prayer and reflection. Record additional insights you discovered that were not addressed in the assignment.

Day 2 – Proverbs 26 – Another View

Something to Consider

I was curious how many times the terms, lips, tongue, mouth and word/s are used in the entire book of Proverbs. I counted 110 combined times. Don't quote me on this. I am sure I missed several and admittingly my eyes blurred at chapter 25. The point is that 100+ times in 31 chapters must be a big deal and it's worth our time to search for them as hidden treasures once again.

"He who speaks truth declares righteousness, but a false witness, deceit. There is one who speaks like the piercings of a sword, but the tongue of the wise promotes health. The truthful lips shall be established forever, but a lying tongue is but for a moment."

Proverbs 12:17-19.

What words or phrases have taken root in your mind and heart these past several weeks, if not these?

Except for a few new topics addressed in chapters 27-31, the topics presented moving forward are primarily repetitions designed by the Holy Spirit through Solomon to penetrate the surface of our mind and bring about change in our lives, challenging us to dig deeper into his Word.

Today will be another opportunity to test and challenge your understanding and personal growth using the topics of your choice presented in Proverbs 26 as a starting point. Feel free to reference back to previous week's cross references that address what comes to your mind or search out different passages of Scripture that speak to the topic/s you are choosing.

If you wrote a letter or made commitments to the Lord at the beginning of part 1 or 2 of this study, now would be a good time to think about them as you spend this time doing your own study.

Something to Pray

Heavenly Father, lead me as I seek to learn and spend time searching your Word as I would hidden treasures. Lord, show me areas that I need to push past what I already know and open my eyes to your loving character in greater ways. In the name of Jesus, amen.

Proverbs 26 – Another View

Note the principle you are researching from Proverbs 26, then note the cross references (past or new) that support how you have grown and the new insight you received from your study. Choose 2 principles.

1) Principle # 1:

a. Passage that supports the evidence of growth. Give an example:

b. Passage that provides new insight. Give an example:

2) Principle # 2:

a. Passage that supports the evidence of growth. Give an example:

b. Passage that provides new insight. Give an example:

3) Overall, how have you seen your growth impact your home life, work life and church life?

4) How are you encouraged or challenged by this exercise?

Proverbs 26 – Closing Thought

"As a dog returns to its vomit, so a fool repeats his foolishness."

Proverbs 26:11.

You've just finished eating your favorite meal, you are full, but unable to resist the mouth-watering dessert. Twenty minutes later, however, your stomach cramps up and as hard as you try, you can't hold back the inevitable and it's now in front of you, only it doesn't look as appetizing as it did originally.

Picture this: Instead of cleaning up and walking away. You grab a straw and happily drink it. How ridiculous and sickening is this thought? My guess is you would never do this, but this is exactly what Proverbs 26:11 is describing. The returning to vomit is not just staring at it but partaking of it.

It serves as a harsh and disgusting picture of what it means when we go back to false and ungodly beliefs, thoughts and behaviors that are generally brought on by life's experiences. The call to growing in wisdom challenges us to stay on the straight path to renewing our mind, but it also includes an equally strong call not to go backwards. When we do, it is unhealthy and the thought of going back should bring this visual to mind. There are many New Testament passages that share this same idea.

May we be women who continually move forward and regain our footing when we begin to stumble and remember that wisdom not only gives a way of escape, but it is also The Way of escape.

Related passages: 2 Corinthians 5:17; 2 Peter 2:20-22

Close out the day with prayer and reflection. Record additional insights you discovered that were not addressed in the assignment.

"Let my cry come before You, O LORD; Give me understanding according to Your word. Let my supplication come before You; deliver me according to Your word."

Psalm 119:169–170.

Day 3 – Proverbs 27

Something to Consider

Ever been so full you are not tempted to eat your favorite dessert? Just thinking about it makes you sick? Or when you are hungry a stale cracker sounds good? What is your favorite season? Can you find something good about your least favorite?

The quality of our lives, and how they are affected, are determined by our levels of contentment. These are the main themes of this chapter, and each fragmented thought and principle speak to them.

Like chapter 26, chapter 27 does not mention the name of the Lord, though we see strong examples of his sovereignty and character on display in the nuggets of wisdom laid out in each verse. As we walk in wisdom, others will see something in us that is genuine and different, which can open the doors for sharing the gospel with others. On the other hand, if we choose our old foolish ways, we will not be a proper reflection of Christ, and unfortunately what will be seen is the wickedness of our hearts.

"As in water face reflects face, so a man's heart reveals the man."
Proverbs 27:19.

If we seek to be full of wisdom, we won't be tempted to go after other things that will only be like bitter water to our soul. Let's find contentment in every season of life. As we pursue these virtues, we will make our Father's heart glad because he will have good things to say of us when the enemy goes before him to accuse and defame us, as Solomon hoped he could do for his son (Proverbs 27:11).

Something to Pray

Father, help me get my fill from wise pursuits and be content with each season of life, whether a time of want or plenty. May I be like Paul and say that I have learned the secret of being content knowing that with you all things are possible because you are the one who supplies all my needs according to your riches in Christ Jesus. Thank you, Lord. Amen.

Proverbs 27
The Big Picture

Read Proverbs chapter 27, then answer the following questions.

1) List 3 attributes of God you see throughout this chapter. List the verse and attribute seen.

a.

b.

c.

2) Walk through each verse and list them under the category that seems most fitting.

Relationships   Contentment/lack of   Seasons

3) Which area are you most challenged by and what do you think is the cause?

4) What is one thing you can do differently to grow in your area of challenge?

Deeper Reflection

"As iron sharpens iron, so a man sharpens the countenance of his friend."
Proverbs 27:17.

At this point we've all read and heard about how God created us for relationships and why it's important in every area of our lives and in sharing the gospel. And yet, here we are again.

There are millions of Christians who stand on deceitful thinking that they can be a Christian without fellowship or sharing God's Word. If that were so, our lives and churches would be free of heartbreak and isolation. I may catch flack for this, but the saying, "Preach the gospel always. When necessary, use words", couldn't be further from the truth. Preaching the gospel, to ourselves, one another and the unsaved must include words. Otherwise, how does God get the credit for doing good things? And how are we to do all the Lord commands about relationships without using words of encouragement or correction? It can't be done. Let's welcome the reminder and challenge in this area of our lives.

This principle is stated throughout the Bible and is a commandment, not suggestion. Therefore, we will spend a little more time on other passages that reinforce and show how Proverbs 27:17 is lived out in practical ways.

1) Read the following passages and note how they add insight to Proverbs 27:17.

a. Ecclesiastes 4:9-12:

b. Acts 2:42-47:

c. Hebrews 10:24-25:

2) Do you need to grow in this area? What could you do differently going forward?

Close out the day with prayer and reflection. Record additional insights you discovered that were not addressed in the assignment.

Have you committed one or two of the repeated cross references or proverbs verses to memory? I would encourage you to do that if you haven't already.

"Let the word of Christ dwell in you richly, teaching and admonishing one another in all wisdom, singing psalms and hymns and spiritual songs, with thankfulness in your hearts to God."

Colossians 3:16 (ESV).

Day 4 – Proverbs 27 – Another View

Something to Consider

"A continual dripping on a rainy day and a contentious woman are alike; Whoever restrains her restrains the wind, and grasps oil with his right hand."

Proverbs 27:15-16.

For the 6th time, the quarrelsome/contentious woman is mentioned. There are many things we learn about her. The first thing being, she is not a woman living in wisdom. Secondly, she enjoys a good argument. It's foolishness at its best. Like many other repeated topics, this one will always be a challenge for us. Or should I say, me?

In my before Christ days, there was nothing that brought me more pleasure than conflict. I thrived off and in it. Having the last word at any cost was my goal. It appeared to serve me well in my self-protecting days, but looking back, it only caused more damage and affected my relationships in destructive ways. My closest friends knew they could count on me to stand up and fight for them, until they crossed me. I had mastered the art of continual dripping...

Of all the other references, this one is followed by what sounds like a challenge and pointless attempt for the one who seeks to restrain this behavior. It's more of warning that any attempt to do so is futile. As futile as trying to restrain the wind or take hold of an object with grease-filled hands.

The only one capable restraining the wind is the One who created it. If we choose wisdom, we will be honest and ask ourselves what the behavior is doing for us. What is the "why" behind it, and to surrender all to the Lord because he is the only one who can work in our hearts to free us from those things that are keeping us in a state of contention.

In this context, Solomon is referring to a married woman, but the principle applies to all people, men and women in any stage of life.

Today we will look at a few passages that give us a broader perspective on the subject. May we recognize that it's a matter of our hearts' beliefs and give us cause to address them.

Something to Pray

Heavenly Father, open my eyes to see any areas where I am resisting you and sitting in a contentious mindset. Help me to renew my mind with the filling of your Word and the healing you offer when I come to you with my anxious thoughts and self-protective ways. In the name of Jesus, amen.

Proverbs 27 – Another View

1) Read the following passages and note how they add insight to Proverbs 27:15-16. Give an example of how you see this in action in your life and loved ones.

a. Proverbs 26:21:

b. 1 Timothy 3:1-7:

2) Look up 3 additional references in the book of Proverbs about contentious/quarrelsome women. Note the verse and give a practical example of this from your own life or as witnessed in another person.

a.

b.

c.

3) How do you see wounds and resentments affecting this behavior? What might you need to change, and how does this give you insight into why others live in this behavior?

Proverbs 27 – Closing Thought

"A stone is heavy and sand is weighty, but a fool's wrath is heavier than both of them."

Proverbs 27:3.

Wisdom always offers a way of escape. We have seen many of them laid out for us in each chapter. Some are simple and practical statements that don't require much thought at all, but others, like verse three is one worth pondering.

Proverbs 27 has a lot to say about healthy relationships and what it takes to have them, and escaping old wounds appears to be the foundation for building them. Read Proverbs 27:3 and then read the entire chapter again. Can you see it?

When we carry heavy burdens and hold tight to sandbags of pain, it will cause us to make foolish decisions. This in turn causes us to behave in ways that pull us deeper into the pit and have far heavier consequences than the original wounds.

Jesus and the writer of Hebrews make this same point.

"Then Jesus said, "Come to me, all of you who are weary and carry heavy burdens, and I will give you rest. Take my yoke upon you. Let me teach you, because I am humble and gentle at heart, and you will find rest for your souls. For my yoke is easy to bear, and the burden I give you is light."

Matthew 11:28-30.

"Therefore we also, since we are surrounded by so great a cloud of witnesses, let us lay aside every weight, and the sin which so easily ensnares us, and let us run with endurance the race that is set before us".

Hebrews 12:1.

Have you memorized these two passages that have been sprinkled throughout this study? Scratch that. Have you come to believe them in the deepest part of your heart? Wisdom points us to the God of all creation and the Savior of hearts, minds and souls. May we receive it, believe it and live it in greater ways all the days of our lives.

Related passage: Romans 13:12-14

Close out the day with prayer and reflection. Record additional insights you discovered that were not addressed in the assignment.

"I am warning you ahead of time, dear friends. Be on guard so that you will not be carried away by the errors of these wicked people and lose your own secure footing. Rather, you must grow in the grace and knowledge of our Lord and Savior Jesus Christ."

2 Peter 3:17–18 (NLT).

Day 5 – Proverbs 28

Something to Consider

The wicked fear everything and nothing. They are led by fear and seek to rule with fear. This truth is threaded throughout the book of Proverbs. Sometimes subtly and other times, plainly. The same principle applies to the righteous.

"The wicked flee when no one pursues, but the righteous are bold as a lion."

Proverbs 28:1.

"He who is of a proud heart stirs up strife, but he who trusts in the LORD will be prospered."

Proverbs 28:25.

Consider these two thoughts as you read through this chapter and give yourself permission to explore all of life's choices laid out before you now and at different seasons of your life. How can these principles explain the world around you?

One of the beautiful aspects of so many proverbs is that they are not theological or absolute truths that we need to keep in complete context so that we are not led astray. They are meant to encourage thoughts and probabilities so that we can live a full and holy life as God intends for his children.

Something to Pray

Heavenly Father, help me to see the principles laid out for me today. Holy Spirit, spark thought in my mind so I can see how fear governs and creates in me the need to control my environment and other people. Help me trust you and surrender all my "what if" thoughts that cause me to flee when no one is pursuing. In the name of Jesus, amen.

Proverbs 28
The Big Picture

Read Proverbs chapter 28, then answer the following questions.

1) Make a list of 2 choices available to the wicked and the righteous and give a practical example from everyday life, yours or in the world around you.

The Wicked

Choice/Behavior
a.

Practical example

b.

The Righteous

Choice/Behavior
a.

Practical example

b.

2) How are you encouraged and challenged in this season of life?

Deeper Reflection

Some have wondered why the question "How are you encouraged and challenged?" "It's too broad", they say. "That's the point", is the gentle reply.

Growing in grace and knowledge of our Lord Jesus Christ requires our own thinking and renewing of our mind, and while God is good to give us pastors and teachers who are called to equip the saints (Ephesians 4:12), what the Apostle John says is especially and much more significantly true:

"But you have an anointing from the Holy One, and you know all things. I have not written to you because you do not know the truth, but because you know it, and that no lie is of the truth."

1 John 2:20-21.

One of the goals of this study was draw attention to the gift and purpose of wisdom for our lives so that we can grow in understanding of God's Word, which would cause us to trust God with all our will.

A secondary goal or prayed outcome would be to stretch our thinking of the many one-liner Solomonisms we read and apply them to our lives. First, to effect change in us, and secondly, to pass them on to the body of Christ and hurting world in attitude and action.

Spend a little bit more time challenging yourself to greater thinking and insight by going back to previous chapters that seem to be coming to your mind more than others. Use them as an opportunity to see if your answers to the "What encourages and challenges you most" questions would change or deepen. From today, through chapter 31, you will be challenged to seek out unfamiliar passages that add insight to the chapter at hand.

1) Look back through part 1, chapters 1-17 of this study and choose 2 topics that encouraged and challenged you most. Answer the question the encourage/challenge question, or a question of your choice again and look up at least 2 new to you cross-references that add insight to the topics you chose. Use Google search or a concordance to research passages on the same theme.

a. Week _____, Topic: Proverbs _____, verse _____ Question

_____

Original answer:

Current answer:

Cross reference 1 _____   Cross reference 2 _____

New insight:

New encouragement and challenge:

b. Week _____, Topic: Proverbs _____, verse _____ Question
_____

Original answer:

Current answer:

Cross reference 1 _____   Cross reference 2 _____

New insight:

New encouragement and challenge:

Close out the day with prayer and reflection. Record additional insights you discovered that were not addressed in the assignment.

"And it is my prayer that your love may abound more and more, with knowledge and all discernment,"

Philippians 1:9.

Day 6 – Another View

Something to Consider

"He who covers his sins will not prosper, but whoever confesses and forsakes them will have mercy."

Proverbs 28:13.

There are multiple reasons we cover our sin, but they all come down to two primary reasons: rebellion or shame. Both will cause a soul to die. For the wicked one who has no desire for repentance and restoration, their death and barren life will end with eternal separation from God. For the righteous, it will lead to a lifestyle of unhealthy coping behaviors causing us to live as though we are dead.

The promise of mercy in the second half of the verse comes from the character of God. When we confess and turn from our sinful actions or coping behaviors we will have mercy. That mercy restores our whole being to freedom.

Prosperity in this principle does not refer to outward blessings directly, though it can include it as an outcome for wise living. The Hebrews would most likely understand its relation to God's blessing for obedience. According to grace, however, this can also relate to the riches gained in freedom from a guilty conscience and in knowing God is faithful and just to forgive and restore the wounded soul. The wounds sin brings on us, whether our own choices, or what others have done to us, weigh us down and we are unable to move forward in faith.

Today we will look at several passages that reveal the truth and what we can learn from them about guilt, shame, depression, and freedom.

"For we do not have a High Priest who cannot sympathize with our weaknesses, but was in all points tempted as we are, yet without sin. Let us therefore come boldly to the throne of grace, that we may obtain mercy and find grace to help in time of need."

Hebrews 4:15-16.

Something to Pray

Father, I confess there are times in the past or even now that I withhold confession for the areas I have stayed in control and not trusted you with my deepest wounds or sin. You promised you would not withhold mercy from me and still, I hesitate at times. Help me to see your goodness and choose to live in freedom and healing. In the name of Jesus, amen.

Proverbs 28 – Another View

1) Read the following passages and note what you learn about hiding, withholding, and freedom.

a. Lamentations 3:22-23:

b. Psalm 51:1-9:

c. Psalm 32:1-9:

d. Acts 3:19:

2) Search out 3 additional passages that speak to the prosperity of the soul when confession and repentance are made.

a.

b.

c.

3) How are you encouraged and challenged by the above passages.

Proverbs 28 – Closing Thought

What are your closing thoughts? Whether in a group study, or individually, it's always a good time to recap what you have read. This helps to organize thoughts and what you've learned and to meditate on the areas God is calling you to grow in, as well as a time to rejoice in how you've grown in at least one of the topics discussed in your study time.

Today, it's your turn. Read Proverbs 28 and then write a personal summary based on your insights. Take a brave step and share it in your discussion time if you are in a group study.

My Closing Thought:

Related passages: Romans chapter 8

Close out the day with prayer and reflection. Record additional insights you discovered that were not addressed in the assignment.

Do you have any unconfessed wounds or sins? Do not go any further. Now would be a good time to lay them boldly before the throne of God so that your soul may prosper and bless those around you.

" I called on Your name, O LORD, From the lowest pit. You have heard my voice:"Do not hide Your ear from my sighing, from my cry for help. You drew near on the day I called on You, And said, "Do not fear!" O Lord, You have pleaded the case for my soul; You have redeemed my life."
Lamentations 3:55-58.

Day 7

Reflect on this week's assignments and note any additional thoughts below. For group studies, choose 1 or 2 questions from each day and discuss as a group and record your thoughts and/or prayer requests.

Week Five

She CALLS US to MARRIAGE

Proverbs 29-31

Day 1 – Proverbs 29

Something to Consider

WORSHIP = Showing fear and reverence, giving devotion in surrender and submission of oneself in trust to something or someone.

From the beginning of part 1 (Proverbs 1-17) and through week 4 of part 2, we have focused on how the beliefs of the heart determine our ability to trust God with all our will and how our will affects our choices for wisdom or folly.

For these last three proverbs, the focus will shift to how trusting God with all our will works together with wisdom or foolishness in whom and what we worship.

Worship isn't only joining other believers in a church service for communion in song, the hearing of the Word and partaking of the Lord's supper. Though components of worship, the Bible teaches something much stronger and deeper than those three things. It's primarily a lifestyle of what or who we bow to and trust. It's an act of surrendering self and giving ourselves over to something or someone else, fully accepting what it/he/she has to offer.

As you read through this chapter, consider how these contrasts reveal a choice in whom or what is being worshipped.

Something to Pray

Father, I have learned a lot, and I'm thankful for the opportunities that have come up that challenge me to put these lessons into practice. But I don't want to get complacent. Give me greater insight into what these repeated statements mean and how I can apply them to my life when I choose to worship you and not my selfish ways. In the name of Jesus, amen.

Proverbs 29
The Big Picture

Read Proverbs chapter 29, then answer the following questions.

1) List 2 actions seen in this chapter that display an act of worship. Note the verses and why you chose them.

a.

b.

2) List 2 actions that represent an act of defiance. Note the verses and why you chose them.

3) Read 2 Chronicles 36:11-16. How do you see Proverbs 28:1 in action.

4) How has Proverbs 28:1 been active in your life in different seasons? Could it be active now with something the Lord is clearly calling you to surrender? What are you learning?

Deeper Reflection

By now, you have read several recurring themes and verses that are repeated word for word, or very close. Have you been tempted to gloss over them as I have, thinking about how that was already addressed? What about bypassing completely without giving it much thought? It's important that we be honest with ourselves, and God about our attitude because when we are, then we will open our hearts and mind to learning once again.

Some of the recurring themes or statements that have hit my heart more than others are:

"A fool vents all his feelings, but a wise man holds them back."

Proverbs 29:11.

It carries the idea of the lack of self-control and speaking without thinking, or sharing my thoughts and feelings, with no intention of resolving the issue or issues at hand. The truth is nothing goes away until there are resolution and reconciliation between God and self. Resolution between other people isn't always possible. A wise person will think before they verbally vomit and will only do so under the right circumstances with the intent of resolving conflict or healing from wounds; old or current.

The second theme that has stood out to me is:

"Where there is no revelation, the people cast off restraint; but happy is he who keeps the law."

Proverbs 29:18.

Proverbs 29:18 reflect the teachings woven through all 31 chapters, and that is the idea of remaining flexible and teachable by having an attitude of humility and a hunger for wisdom, knowledge and understanding.

What has been speaking loudest to you? Spend a little more time today reflecting on two themes in this chapter and doing some research of your own.

1) List two recurring themes and why you chose them. Note all the chapters and verses in which you find them.

a. Theme #1 _____

_____

b. Chapter/Verse _____

_____

c. Theme #2 _____

_____

d. Chapter/Verse _____

_____

2) What is it about these two themes that gained your attention most?

3) Research 1 cross reference for each of the themes, note them and how they add insight to what you have already learned.

a. Theme #1 cross reference:

b. Theme #2 cross reference:

4) How are you challenged by Proverbs 29, and why?

Close out the day with prayer and reflection. Record additional insights you discovered that were not addressed in the assignment.

"Many seek the ruler's favor, but justice for man comes from the Lord."
Proverbs 29:26.

Day 2 - Proverbs 29 - Another View

Something to Consider

The Lord is so good to send his Holy Spirit to teach us when we faithfully seek him on a personal level.

Studying the Bible with others is essential for growth, accountability and encouragement. I'm always encouraged when I study with other women and hear what they have to say from their perspective on the same truths being discussed. It's equally important to study for ourselves to see what God is revealing to each of us for our season of life.

This study is a good example. There is so much to learn from each chapter, and as the author, I can only come at it from what the Spirit is leading and teaching me in. Though the Holy Spirit led me to ask specific questions and cite cross-references, I haven't touched on every point for every person. Some passages are more impactful than others. In fact, I am sure there have been several times you may have wished I addressed a verse or theme more deeply than what is presented, or that a particular verse was discussed but completely passed over, leaving you with a sense of disappointment. You may not have understood my perspective or why particular cross-references were chosen. Praise the Lord if this is the case, because that is an indicator that you are hungry to learn and grow.

Today you can walk through Proverbs 29 focusing on what is important to you. Feel free to use the pattern shown in this workbook or use a different method familiar to you. Another option is to simply read it and ask the Lord to give insight and direct you to other passages that speak to the same subject for each verse that provokes thought.

Research and looking for wisdom as hidden treasure is the call for today, just as Proverbs 1-7 instructs us to do.

Something to Pray

Holy Spirit, show me something I need to see. Remind me of what I have forgotten. Thank you, heavenly Father for the gift of Jesus and your Spirit. In the name of Jesus, amen.

Proverbs 29 – Another View

1) Read Proverbs 29, then fill in the blanks with 1 – 2 verses that piqued your interest.

a. Verse _____

My understanding:

Cross References:

a.

b.

My summary:

b. Verse _____

My understanding:

Cross References:

a.

b.

My summary:

Proverbs 29 – Closing Thought

God's throne is established forever. Nothing takes him by surprise. Because we live in a fallen world, bad and painful things will happen. As women who are growing in wisdom, we can choose to a part of the righteous that will make a difference in our sphere of influence. We have been given a tremendous gift to be among the saints of God. May we live accordingly and never grow weary of doing good in the sight of the Lord and never tire of growing in wisdom and knowledge.

My prayer and hope is that I will not delay in shifting my thoughts and actions to God's purpose when the Spirit makes truth known to me. How about you?

"And as He walked by the Sea of Galilee, He saw Simon and Andrew his brother casting a net into the sea; for they were fishermen. Then Jesus said to them, "Follow Me, and I will make you become fishers of men." They immediately left their nets and followed Him."

Mark 1:16-18.

What will choosing wisdom and worship through obedience cost you? What is Jesus calling each of us to leave behind and immediately follow him?

Related passages: James chapter 1

Close out the day with prayer and reflection. Record additional insights you discovered that were not addressed in the assignment.

"And let us not grow weary while doing good, for in due season we shall reap if we do not lose heart."

Galatians 6:9.

Day 3 – Proverbs 30

Something to Consider

This chapter differs from all the others because the author uses himself as an example of what wisdom and humility looks like in the opening statement. He speaks of himself briefly, then moves to worship, and into a poetic style using numeric groupings of topics to provoke thought and wonder, rather than contrasting statements.

It can be divided into 4 main sections to assist in understanding and personal application.

1. Humility, worship and praise
2. Generations of the wicked
3. List of wonders
4. Call to silence foolishness

In some ways, Proverbs chapter 30 gathers all the teachings throughout the first 29 chapters, inviting us to become one with wisdom and prepares us for the complete picture of wisdom principles laid out by King Lemuel's mother in Proverbs 31.

It's also interesting that the only thing we learn about Agur is that he is the son of Jakeh, whom we also don't know anything about. As well as his friends, Ithiel and Ucal. The point is what he had to say is more important than knowing the specifics of his life. My guess is that this letter was pulled from a compilation of Agur's writings. The point is what he had to say is not as important as knowing specifics about his life. His message shows he was humble and a man of worship who was well acquainted with God and the words spoken through the prophets and of Israel's history. We also see the hand of the Holy Spirit spurring thoughts in him that are addressed in the New Testament.

This is something we can remind ourselves of: our accomplishments or status may not go down in history for all to know, but our lifestyle of worship through wisdom will make a difference to those in our corner of the world. It's far better for us to leave a legacy that has eternal value, instead of worldly accolades.

Something to Pray

Father, humble me in the areas that are needed. Give me a hunger to pursue what is most valuable to you and help me ponder these sayings from your servant of past times, Agur. Show me what you want me to see. In the name of Jesus, amen.

Proverbs 30
The Big Picture

Read Proverbs chapter 30, then answer the following questions.

1) What is the evidence of Agur's humility and vulnerability? What is he measuring himself against? How does this challenge you and where you believe you are in your walk with God?

2) How are you challenged by his questions (rhetorical or not) in verse 4? In what ways do they offer worship?

3) What do you learn about God's word and what is the warning? How does this speak to worship and humility?

4) What is his prayer in verses 7-9? List 2-3 wisdom principles seen throughout the book of Proverbs that are present in his requests.

5) What is Agur's challenge and warning in verse 32-33? What is the Holy Spirit challenging you with in this chapter?

Deeper Reflection

Every generation comes with its own unique set of challenges: the economy, political climate and pop-culture to name a few. Within each, people have a choice to run with the crowd and world's way or to go the way of wisdom.

Each generation mentioned by Agur captures several principles of the foolish that are spread throughout chapters 1-29.

Let's spend some time looking at these more closely.

1) Read Proverbs 30:11-14. Choose 1 of the 4 generations mentioned, then research other statements in previous chapters that give examples of the descriptions and list at least 1.

Example:
Generation: Vs 11 – There is a generation that curses (dishonors or disgraces) his father.
Scripture reference and my understanding: Proverbs 19:13 - "A foolish son is a grief to his father." When I make a foolish decision, it can grieve and disgrace my father if he's taught me and nurtured me well. It shows I didn't listen to his wise counsel.

Generation:

Scripture reference and my understanding:

2) What else comes to your mind as you read this section of the chapter?

Close out the day with prayer and reflection. Record additional insights you discovered that were not addressed in the assignment.

Passages that speak to honoring or bringing disgrace to our fathers and mothers can be difficult and confusing for those who have been spiritually, emotionally and/or physically abused by their parents. It is important to understand that the principles laid out in Proverbs and the rest of Scripture are related to a healthy (not perfect) family. We do not have to obey or appease our parents' demands when they are abusive and expect us to satisfy their wishes based on their own sinful behaviors and unfulfilled lives. What we can do is be honoring by living a life of faith and serving the Lord and forgiving them for their treatment toward us. Forgiveness does not demand reconciliation with abusers. Wisdom principles apply as their acts of abuse are reflective of them being under the influence of the enemy and living in folly as described in the first 7 chapters of Proverbs. If you need support in this area to work through the pain and confusion, please reach out to me at Teresa@riseupcfw.com.

Day 4 – Proverbs 30 – Another View

Something to Consider

In verses 15-31, Agur uses the same pattern as God instructed Amos, the farmer, to use when he called him to prophesy to Israel during a time of flourishing for the nation. The warning was regarding what was to come because they had begun to grow complacent, and greed and injustice were coming to the surface.

This gives me another reason to believe Agur had a close relationship with God and was familiar with his laws for his children as spoken through other prophets and wise men.

"Thus says the LORD: for three transgressions of Damascus, and for four...."
Amos 1:3.

"There are three things that are never satisfied, four never say, 'enough!'"
Proverbs 30:15b.

These two men that we know little about should again remind us that we don't have to be teachers, have an elevated status or be formally educated with degrees to be a wise and good example to others. We all are capable of knowing God's Word well and implementing it into our lives. It only takes seeking it out with our whole heart.

Proverbs 30:15-31 give us the perfect opportunity to slow down and think about what is being said and challenge ourselves to search the Scriptures in the Old and New Testament for examples or similar passages that point us in the direction of wisdom. We have promises that we will find it when we put God's Word into practice.

This will be our focus today.

Something to Pray

Father, give me courage to step out of my comfort zone of what is already familiar to me from your Word. Help me slow down and consider what is being said in these passages. Holy Spirit, lead me to new passages and insight so that I may grow in the grace and knowledge of my Lord Jesus Christ and be a faithful witness in my family and community. In the name of Jesus, amen.

Proverbs 30 – Another View

1) Read Proverbs 30:15-31. Choose 2 of the 5 segments related to the "three things, four" pattern (verses 15-19, 21-31). Note the verse number and write it out along with each of the four things mentioned. Next to the four things, write out what thoughts/passages are prompted and then research 1 new passage that adds insight to those thoughts.

Verse #:

a.

b.

c.

d.

Verse #:

a.

b.

c.

d.

Proverbs 30 – Closing Thought

"If you have been foolish in exalting yourself, or if you have devised evil, put your hand on your mouth: For as the churning of milk produces butter, and the wringing of the nose produces blood, so the forcing of wrath produces strife."

Proverbs 30:32-33.

If I've learned anything from the book of Proverbs, it's that humility is wise and essential to trusting the Lord with all my will and is the beginning of my ability to worship God in spirit and truth as Jesus commands.

Help me, Lord to put a muzzle over my mouth when all that wants to pour out of me is pride! Beyond that, Father, help me open my hands and offer my pride to you as a sacrifice of praise. In the name of Jesus, amen.

May we choose to be a generation that does not seek its own wisdom. May we be women who do not devour one another and stab each other in the back with our words. Let's be women who pour out grace where there is judgment and offer a hand up in mercy in time of need.

Finally, I am reminded of the importance of being content. There is so much wisdom in this because it will keep us focused on godly and eternal pursuits, whether we gain notoriety in this world or not. It helps me to keep worldly gains in perspective while teaching me not to be lazy.

"Now godliness with contentment is great gain. For we brought nothing into this world, and it is certain we can carry nothing out. And having food and clothing, with these we shall be content....Command those who are rich in this present age not to be haughty, nor to trust in uncertain riches but in the living God, who gives us richly all things to enjoy. Let them do good, that they may be rich in good works, ready to give, willing to share."

1 Timothy 6:6-8, 17-18.

Related passages: Job 38; Psalm 12; John 17:17

Close out the day with prayer and reflection. Record additional insights you discovered that were not addressed in the assignment.

"Oh, that men would give thanks to the LORD for His goodness, and for His wonderful works to the children of men! For He satisfies the longing soul, and fills the hungry soul with goodness."

Psalm 107:8-9.

Day 5 — Proverbs 31

Something to Consider

Proverbs 31! Did you think you would ever get here? It has taken many weeks to arrive, but I hope you have experienced and recognized that is was a good and necessary road. In chapter 1, day 1's Something to Consider section, I stated the following:

> In chapters 1–3, we are introduced to Wisdom in the feminine. It speaks to the relational part of God's character and contrasts wisdom with folly. In a sense, wisdom acts as the voice of the Holy Spirit since he is the one who convicts, corrects, comforts, and leads us in our walk with God.
>
> Each chapter thereafter will continue to lead us to the call to join as one with wisdom in all her fullness and when we do, we will be prepared to walk in the Spirit in greater ways. Chapter 31 ends with the personification of wisdom in an analogy of a man finding a virtuous wife—virtues we will find are taught throughout the first 30 Proverbs and apply to men as well. In fact, to all believers in whatever stage of life we find ourselves.
>
> The invitation to all of us is to become one with wisdom as pictured in a husband-and-wife relationship and in relation to being united with Christ. As you walk through this study, keep in mind that wisdom speaks first to the character of God and secondly to what we can learn and apply to our lives.

Each chapter is rich with instruction and insight into the benefits of wise choices. With many of them fresh in our minds, we will see how they are laid out in chapter 31.

King Lemuel's mother speaks to her son about wise choices for himself, essentially summing up the strong points of the first 7 chapters, relating to the immoral woman (Satan), following by instructions on what kind of wife she would have for him: Stay away from the immoral woman and move toward and remain with the wisdom. Her encouragement coupled with the knowledge that God always referred to Israel as his wife, and the church being the bride of Christ should help us see and hear this call to be united with wisdom.

Something to Pray

Father, thank you for all you have shown me through your Word. Help me to continue to grow in wisdom, and practice with every opportunity that comes my way. Give me a hunger for more of you and to keep studying and learning to trust you with my will in greater ways. In the name of Jesus, amen.

Proverbs 31
The Big Picture

Read Proverbs chapter 31, then answer the following questions.

1) Compare Proverbs 31:1-9 with Proverbs 1 and 2. List 3 principles King Lemuel's mother expresses that Solomon expressed to his son? How does this point to worship and unity with God and his wisdom?

a.

b.

c.

2) How do his choices pave the way to finding a virtuous wife or living with/for the immoral woman?

3) Does her advice apply to women? (Consider the broad audience Proverbs is directed toward). Explain your answer using a practical example.

4) What passages or lessons come to mind from previous chapters, and how has your understanding increased since then.

Deeper Reflection

For some of you, the idea of Proverbs 31:10-31 being the culmination of wisdom in action is new and it may be creating a lot of suspicion and confusion, or bring on a big a sigh of relief. Before moving forward, let's spend a little more time reflecting on our thoughts and feelings on this topic. It can help with our willingness to trust God with our will and bring us to a deeper level of worship by being honest with our thoughts.

Read verses 10-31, then answer the following questions.

1) How have you viewed this section of Scripture in the past, and how do you view it now?

2) What thoughts come to mind? Be completely honest with yourself and the Lord.

3) What feelings have your thoughts brought up, and how has this affected your walk with God?

4) How has this study encouraged and challenged your thinking and understanding of Proverbs 31?

Close out the day with prayer and reflection. Record additional insights you discovered that were not addressed in the assignment.

"Wisdom has built her house, she has hewn out her seven pillars; She has slaughtered her meat, she has mixed her wine, she has also furnished her table. She has sent out her maidens, she cries out from the highest places of the city, "Whoever is simple, let him turn in here!" As for him who lacks understanding, she says to him, "Come, eat of my bread and drink of the wine I have mixed. Forsake foolishness and live, and go in the way of understanding."

Proverbs 9:1-6.

Day 6 – Proverbs 31 – Another View

Something to Consider

"Who can find a virtuous wife? For her worth is far above rubies."
Proverbs 31:10.

Focusing attention on the wife's specific behaviors while referring to a model of wisdom may be distracting for some. A married woman who puts these skills into practice is a gift to her husband and she will gain honor and praise. But assigning this list of attributes to a literal wife and expecting her performance to achieve them has caused a lot of harm. It puts a tremendous amount of pressure and stress on a married woman who believes she can't possibly measure up. It has also allowed for spiritual abuse from men and has caused unmarried women to avoid Proverbs 31:10-31 altogether since it is believed to be irrelevant to them. Others have become hyper-focused on certain responsibilities.

When we read the virtuous wife as exemplifying wisdom, we can see the "works" are virtues and qualities rather than a level of performance that a wife must attain. It further reveals these qualities are for every one of God's children, and they are obtained by fearing the Lord.

"Charm is deceitful and beauty is passing but a woman who fears the LORD, shall be praised."
Proverbs 31:30.

Today we will focus on the qualities the behaviors reveal by looking back at previous chapters. You will also have an opportunity to research cross references that add insight to this passage.

Something to Pray

Heavenly Father, thank you for freeing me from the bondage of performance as my measure of whether I am a good wife. Thank you for revealing to me that these are qualities that are for all your children to live and be an example of your character and love. Help me to move forward in you and your wisdom. I entrust areas that I have been hanging on too tightly to and surrender my will to you. I pray my internal actions will be received by you in the form of worship. In the name of Jesus, amen.

Proverbs 31 – Another View

Read Proverbs 31:10-31, then answer the following questions.

1) Listed below are 7 virtues/characteristics on display in this passage that are gained in the fear of the Lord. Under each virtue, write the corresponding verse/s you see that apply or fit the behavior.

a. Integrity:

b. Diligence:

c. Preparedness:

d. Generous:

e. Hard worker / Not lazy:

f. Speaks life:

g. Tends to her own home:

2) What do you learn about God's character in Proverbs 31?

3) Share one practical example of how these virtues belong to all God's people.

4) Read the following cross-references and note how they add insight to Proverbs 31:10-31.

a. Proverbs 13:1-6:

b. Proverbs 14:23:

c. James 3:13:

Pause for a moment and consider various chapters and their topics by skimming through the entire study, parts 1 and 2 that addressed the themes mentioned in Proverbs 31, then answer the questions below.

5) Read 1 chapter of your choice between 1 – 16. Note how it complements chapter 31. What stands out to you the most and how are you encouraged?

6) Read 1 chapter of your choice between 18-30. Note how it complements chapter 31. What stands out to you the most and how are you encouraged?

7) How have your thoughts and feelings changed from day 5 of this week's assignments for chapter 31?

Proverbs 31 – Closing Thought

"Happy is the man who finds wisdom, And the man who gains understanding; For her proceeds are better than the profits of silver, and her gain than fine gold. She is more precious than rubies, and all the things you may desire cannot compare with her. Length of days is in her right hand, in her left hand riches and honor.

Her ways are ways of pleasantness, and all her paths are peace. She is a tree of life to those who take hold of her, and happy are all who retain her."

Proverbs 3:13-18.

I have hope as I consider the ways I have grown over the past several weeks, but it also raises another challenge for me to continue to grow in the virtues laid out throughout the book of Proverbs.

Looking back at chapter 1, Solomon laid out several reasons for his instruction:

- To know wisdom and instruction
- To perceive the words of understanding
- To receive the instruction of wisdom, justice judgment and equity
- To give prudence to the simple, to the young man knowledge and discretion
- To understand a proverb and an enigma, the words of the wise and their riddles

Proverbs 31 is packed with wisdom in action and what it looks like when we learn from Solomon's instruction. How would you rate yourself against his purposes? As daughters of the most high God, may we pursue the principles laid out in this chapter and be source of encouragement to those around us to do the same.

Related passages: Psalm 119

Close out the day with prayer and reflection. Record additional insights you discovered that were not addressed in the assignment.

"Finally, my brethren, be strong in the Lord and the power of His might. Put on the whole armor of God that you may be able to stand against the wiles of the devil."

Ephesians 6:10.

Day 7

Reflect on this week's assignments and note any additional thoughts below. For group studies, choose 1 or 2 questions from each day and discuss as a group and record your thoughts and/or prayer requests.

Dear friends,

My hope and prayer is that you have come away from this study with greater understanding of God's Word and have a deeper level of trust in him as we looked at Proverbs from an emotional and relational perspective. May God multiply your faith as you go and grow in the grace and knowledge of our Lord Jesus Christ.

Please feel free to reach out with any questions or comments related to this study or if you would like to explore additional coaching and Bible studies by Rise Up.

Grace and peace to you in the name of the Lord,

Teresa

Special thanks to Debby Walker and Cheryl Rogers for their dedication to this work. Your insights, suggestions and edits are invaluable. Thank you for speaking into my life and being a light in the darkness to me and many others!

Thank you to all the women of Grace Community Fellowship who challenge me every day to grow in grace and truth every day.

Thank you to my husband, children and grandchildren who support the work of God in every way. You are my rocks this side of heaven.

About the Author

Teresa Ortiz is an author and speaker, and the founder and director of Rise Up, CFW, Inc. A non-profit organization that exists to support women and teens on the path to healing from trauma and the various coping behaviors that often follow. She is a Certified Trauma Informed Care Practitioner and Certified Life Coach with over 3000 hours of coaching and counseling experience. She is also the director of women's ministries at her local church.

Her greatest joys are spending time with her husband, children and grandchildren and pointing others to Christ for freedom and growth in their relationship with him.

Visit Riseupcfw.com for more information about Rise Up if you have a need for support, or if you would like to support the work we do.

www.ingramcontent.com/pod-product-compliance
Lightning Source LLC
LaVergne TN
LVHW061329060426
835513LV00015B/1337